S0-DVF-841

the Office of the Librarian of Congress, at Washington, D. C.

A. L. Bancroft & Co., Lithographers, San Fran

EW OF
ALIFORNIA

ING SOUTH-WEST.

The County Seat of San Diego County and the proposed Terminus of the Texas Pacific Railroad.   Present Population, about 3,000.   A commercial town; publishes two newspapers, " San Diego Union " and " World," weekly and daily editions.

13. Horton's Hall.	17. Lyon House.	21. Book Store of Schneider & Kuep
14. Telegraph Offices.	18. Bay View Hotel.	22. San Diego Foundry.
15. Horton House.	19. Government Barracks.	23. San Diego Planing Mill.
16. San Diego County Court House.	20. San Diego Flouring Mill.	24. City Brewery.

Yesterday's San Diego

Seemann's Historic Cities Series

NEIL MORGAN & TOM BLAIR

Yesterday's

SAN DIEGO

Seemann's Historic Cities Series No. 21

E. A. Seemann Publishing, Inc.
Miami, Florida

Library of Congress Cataloging in Publication Data

Morgan, Neil Bowen, 1924-
    Yesterday's San Diego.

    (Seemann's historic cities series ; no. 21)
    Bibliography: p.
    Includes index.
    1. San Diego, Calif.--History--Pictorial works.
I. Blair, Tom, joint author.   II.   Title.
F868.S22M67   979.4'98   75-44455
ISBN 0-912458-63-1

Copyright © 1976 by Neil Morgan & Tom Blair
Library of Congress Catalog Card No. 75-44455
ISBN 0-912458-63-1

All rights reserved, including rights of reproduction and use in any form or by any means, including the making of copies by any photo process, or by any electronic or mechanical device, printed or written or oral, or recording for sound or visual reproduction or for use in any knowledge or retrieval system or device, unless permission in writing is obtained from the copyright proprietors.

Manufactured in the United States of America.

Contents

JUAN RODRIGUEZ CABRILLO was the first European to touch the soil of California, landing at Point Loma in 1542. From a painting by Darrel Millsap. (Copley Books)

Preface

IN COMPOSING this pictorial history of San Diego, we have sought to make it more than a book of photographs of a city. On the other hand, we have not attempted to write a definitive history of a city. Within the framework of this book, that would have been impossible. It also would have been unnecessary.

Richard F. Pourade, the premier historian of San Diego, has given the city a rich series of six books that trace the history of San Diego from the landing of Juan Rodrıguez Cabrillo to the city's emergence as a military bastion in World War II. We owe Mr. Pourade a huge debt, for much of the information found in this book was drawn from his years of dedicated research and writings.

A work such as this also would have been impossible had it not been for the extensive library of historical photographs that have been preserved by the Title Insurance and Trust Company of San Diego. With the loving care and rare prescience of Larry Booth, the library's curator, the Title Insurance and Trust Company collection has grown to more than 100,000 negatives and 10,000 prints illustrating San Diego's history.

Additionally, Mr. Booth has spent many hours with the authors, guiding them through the collection and aiding in the best possible selection of representative pictures. We owe him great thanks.

Most of the photographs in this book are from the Historical Collection of Title Insurance and Trust Company, San Diego, California. The photographs are printed with the express approval of Title Insurance and Trust Company, and credit is abbreviated (TI).

Other photo credits are abbreviated as follows: Union-Tribune Publishing Company (UT); Teledyne-Ryan Aeronautical (TR), and Del Mar Thoroughbred Club (DM).

The Union-Tribune Publishing Company has been a valuable source of photographs and historical data. And we wish to express our gratitude to Helen K. Copley for allowing us to draw on that source, and to the Union-Tribune librarians who aided us.

Of great help in identifying photographs and tracing the early history of San Diego has been *The Story of New San Diego and of its Founder, Alonzo E. Horton*, written with care and devotion by Elizabeth C. MacPhail. We thank her.

Thanks go to Don Smith of the Del Mar Thoroughbred Club, who provided information and photographs, and William Wagner of Teledyne-Ryan Aeronautical, who did the same.

Certain introductory pictures are printed with the permission of Copley Books. Reprints of several photographs were provided by Charles Doyle. Thanks also are due to them.

This book grew with the encouragement and patience of family and friends: Judith Morgan, Jill Morgan, Wendy Blair, Virginia Blair, Amy Blair, Kim Doyle, Johnny and Kathy Doyle, Mrs. Robert McIver, and many others.

In addition to the authors whose names appear on the cover, there has been a third author, John C. Doyle. His friendship, hard work, and eagerness to study and record the history of San Diego has been of inestimable value. His dedication and hours of labor over photographs and detail have made this book a far better and more accurate history than it might have been.

NEIL MORGAN and TOM BLAIR

San Diego, 1976

[8]

FATHER JUNIPERO SERRA, founder of California's first mission at San Diego in 1769. From a recent painting by Dr. William J. Doyle.

Yesterday's San Diego

SAN DIEGO is a success story—but a story of success evolving from failures, for San Diego today is the result of unrealized dreams of greatness.

From the beginning, San Diego seemed a more logical setting than Los Angeles or San Francisco for a great metropolis. Our founders and boosters sought desperately to be big and we have still, somehow, not entirely succeeded.

San Diego—not Los Angeles or San Francisco—is the kind of place that those in other parts of the world are most likely to think of when they picture California: sunshine and water, not yet shrouded in smog or grown into anonymous infinity, still full of dreams, still obsessed with the hope of greatness tomorrow.

San Diego is the city where California began, and it intended to be in all ways the first city of California.

But there was little gold in San Diego's hills, and the builders of railroads and highways from the East found better passes through the mountains, leading into San Francisco and Los Angeles. With one of the nation's finest natural harbors, San Diego surrendered maritime supremacy first to San Francisco, then to Los Angeles, when the latter built its own unnatural harbor.

More than fifty years ago, San Diego leaders steadfastly denied ambitions for a booming metropolis, but they hired experts to tell them why the city had failed to boom. They glowered while Los Angeles became a runaway megalopolis, and only now are they beginning to realize that they were blessed by their early failures.

The first inhabitants here were the Indians, and San Diego and the rest of California remained the Indians' land for more than two centuries after the first white man stepped ashore.

Because of the nature of the Baja California peninsula, early Spaniards thought California to be an island. From the center of New Spain at Mexico City, explorers roamed far

THE CROSS IS RAISED on the site of the first California mission on July 16, 1769, at San Diego's Presidio Hill. The painting is by Lloyd Harting.

to the south, into the Andes in search of Inca gold. To the north, they ventured rarely. California was a savage wilderness.

Juan Rodríguez Cabrillo sailed into San Diego Harbor in 1542, becoming the first European to touch the soil of the California of today. There was no thought of colonization then. Cabrillo was the Columbus of California, seeking a northwest passage to link the Atlantic and Pacific. This was the time of Spanish glory on the seas, and the hunt was for quick riches; nothing in the California shoreline suggested wealth. But Cabrillo was high in his praise of the natural harbor of San Diego.

In 1602, Sebastián Vizcaíno named San Diego, Santa Monica, Santa Barbara, and Monterey while sailing along the Southern California coast for Spain. In his log he so embellished the virtues of Monterey as a safe harbor that the next white man on the scene 167 years later, Catalonian nobleman Don Gaspar de Portolá, marched past without recognizing it.

The Catholic Church, with missionary fervor, pleaded through these years for a settlement of California and conversion of its Indians. But the star of Spanish greatness was soon in decline, and a campaign in so remote a region seemed too costly to the Spanish viceroy at Mexico City.

[10]

Prevailing northwest winds blew against explorers who sought to beat their way under sail up the California coast. And overland explorations by the Spanish from Mexico had revealed California to be set apart by desert and precipitous mountains. It was less than inviting.

No ship entered San Diego harbor to disturb the placid indolence of the Indians from Vizcaíno's visit in 1602 until its settlement in 1769.

With reluctance, Spain moved finally toward California. But Spain was intent only on heading off Russian fur traders who were reported sailing out across the Aleutians and down the coast of northwest America. Spain moved forward with the sword and the cross.

A military campaign against hordes of Indians who still lived in the Stone Age seemed unthinkable. It was more reasonable to lend modest military support to mission priests who wished to christianize the heathen, and incidentally hoist the flag of Spain.

A lonely desert string of missions was slowly built up in Mexican Baja California, their outpost about three hundred miles short of today's United States border. The Spanish viceroy assigned José de Gálvez, an Andalusian who had become an adviser to the Spanish king, Charles III, to investigate the Russian menace to California. There was not much menace, but Gálvez saw an opportunity to advance his career.

He sailed to Baja California to organize a force that might settle Monterey, which had been regarded as the prime California site since the glowing reports from Vizcaíno so many years earlier. The Franciscan mission priest, Junípero Serra, had just been named to head the missions of Baja California, and he was eager to push the mission chain northward.

It is hard to imagine a less likely candidate than Serra to survive the ordeals of a desert frontier. When his challenge came, he already was fifty-five years old. He was no more than five feet, three inches, in height. He suffered incessant chest pains as a result of his fervent evangelism, not uncommon in that day: he struck himself with stones and chains as he preached, and held lighted torches to his body.

Serra's legs and feet were given to severe swelling, making him often a near-cripple. He was humble and meek, deprecating his abilities.

Yet his spirit was so intransigent that all who dealt with him knew him as a formidable adversary. A distinguished theologian and teacher of philosophy in his native Mallorca, Serra had abandoned the academic life at the age of thirty-six to become a missionary in Mexico.

Carlos III and José de Gálvez could have had no more intrepid champion in their goal of blocking Russian advances toward California. It did not matter that their interests were divergent; the great crucifix which Serra wore day and night would lead the way, and the Catalonian captain, Don Gaspar de Portolá, would carry the sword. The settling of California hinged on the zeal of Serra and the ambition of Gálvez.

San Diego was chosen as the first California base for the expedition because of its harbor and its position as a halfway point from Loreto to Monterey. Gálvez assigned two overland parties; Serra was to march with Portolá.

Three packet ships were outfitted to sail toward San Diego, and tragedy haunted them all. They bore sailors and soldiers, seed and farm implements, foodstuffs, and cargoes of vestments, sacred vases and ornaments. One ship, the *San José*, vanished. Scurvy prostrated the crews of the *San Antonio* and *San Carlos* during their tedious beat northwestward into the wind.

Leading one of the two overland expeditions, Portolá and Serra came three hundred and fifty miles with soldiers, muleteers, several hundred head of cattle, and a pack train through a desert described by Father Juan Crespi, diarist of the expedition, as "sterile, arid, lacking grass and water, and abounding in stones and thorns."

Portolá had been skeptical of Serra's chances to survive the march, and his fears proved valid. In his diary for May 17, 1769, Serra wrote: "By now the swelling has reached halfway up my leg, which is covered with sores . . . I was afraid that before long I should have to follow the expedition on a stretcher."

The company ran out of food; friendly Indian servants deserted or died. Portolá led his men up into the desert mountains to kill geese and rabbits, and back to the Pacific shore for clams and fish. Water was scarce; they went for three or four days without finding water holes, and their stock went without water for almost twice that long.

After six weeks, Serra saw on the horizon the white sails of the *San Antonio* and *San Carlos* in San Diego harbor. But the tragic little camp he found at the mouth of the San Diego River brought tears to his eyes. The *San Carlos* had wandered lost off the California coast, finally arriving in San Diego after 110 days. Those of its crew who survived scurvy were unfit for duty. Perhaps sixty of about ninety crewmen of the two ships were already dead, and more were dying.

Even ashore, in a land that was soon to grow green with the cultivation of fruits and vegetables, the natural preventive for scurvy, there was no help. Serra and Portolá set to burying their dead and caring for the survivors.

Serra wrote: "I arrived here at the fort of San Diego. It is beautiful to behold and does not belie its reputation. Here I met all who set out before me, whether by sea or by land, but not the dead."

He noted that he had reached his destination in a pagan land among Indians that were shameless in their nudity, "a harvest of souls that might easily be gathered into the bosom of Our Holy Mother the Church and, it would appear, with very little trouble." It was the fervent dream of a missionary, but it bore little resemblance to the terrors that lay ahead.

The Indians were shy, at first, but soon they grew bolder and began to steal—even the sheets off the men dying of scurvy. One party of Indians rowed out to the *San Carlos* and attempted to steal its sails. They did not respond to Serra's evangelism. The soldiers who were able to stand guard built a stockade of simple logs and thatch and watched warily.

Two weeks later Portolá led a group of men he referred to as "skeletons who had been spared by scurvy, hunger, and thirst" on an overland march to seek out Monterey Bay. Serra stayed behind, and on July 16, 1769, he dedicated a small brush wood hut as the first California mission, San Diego de Alcalá.

The *San Antonio* sailed back to San Blas for supplies with eight men aboard, all that remained of her original crew of twenty-eight; only two of these survived the trip to San Blas.

[12]

That first winter almost ended the Spanish effort to colonize California. Food supplies were exhausted. Colonists lived on fish and geese, and what corn they could wheedle out of the Indians in barter. Portolá returned from a grueling and futile march north as far as San Francisco Bay during which he and his men had been reduced to eating their mules.

Early in March 1770, with the little San Diego presidio and mission at a desperate ebb, Portolá set a deadline for abandoning the colony and returning to Mexico unless supplies should arrive. Serra declared that he would not depart under any circumstances. Portolá's deadline approached, and the priest began a novena, a nine-day devotion of prayers.

The final day came and there was no ship on the horizon. Portolá began to prepare for departure. At three in the afternoon, sails were seen on the horizon, moving north. It was the *San Antonio*, on her way with supplies to Monterey, where her captain assumed Portolá had succeeded in establishing a camp. Cheered even by the sight of a passing ship, Portolá agreed to delay his departure. Four days later, in what seemed to Serra an answer to prayer, the *San Antonio* reappeared, this time entering San Diego harbor.

Her crewmen, going ashore for water near Port Conception, had learned from Indians that Portolá's expedition had returned to San Diego. Her supplies saved San Diego. Until his death, Serra celebrated a high mass on the nineteenth of every month in memory of the vigil which preserved the first settlement in California.

Serra, who left San Diego and went about building the chain of twenty-one California missions, was not present on the night of November 5, 1775, when Indians, aroused now to the expulsion of the white man, attacked and burned the mission. Soldiers fought them off, but Serra's successor at San Diego, Father Luis Jayme, was lost. He pushed out into the midnight melee with his hands upraised and called to the Indians, "Love God, my children!" He was clubbed and shot full of arrows, then taken to the river and cut to pieces, the first martyr of California.

By that year, there were five missions and two presidios along a four-hundred mile strip of California coast, and only seventy-five soldiers on guard. It would have been a simple matter then for a united Indian effort to erase all the tedious efforts of a decade, but the Indians of the California coast, softened by a relatively easy existence, were not fighters. Soon they began to drift into the missions as converts, led by gifts, and attracted by singing. When baptized, they moved into the mission compounds and were ruled under rigid regulations. They could not leave the mission community without permission. They were taught the rudiments of Christianity, along with farming and mechanical crafts.

Death came to Junípero Serra in 1784, at the age of seventy, as he clutched the foot-long crucifix he had brought up from Mexico fifteen years before. There were 4,600 Indian converts living at his California missions. The land was held in theoretical trust for the Indians, and Serra's passion for improving the lot of the heathen seemed established on a sound basis. Yet in another fifty years the mission system would be destroyed.

The missions and their vast surrounding farmlands grew verdant with wheat and vine-yards, usually under irrigation. Many priests felt it unseemly to operate great ranches and supervise machine shops, but it seemed necessary to the support of their prime function of winning souls.

The missions developed a powerful commerce, trading hides, tallow, wine, brandy, olive oil, grain, and leatherwork for manufactured goods brought increasingly by trading vessels. Yet the frequent appearance of Yankee ships from New England suggested the doom of California as a Spanish colony.

From the start, historic tides caused sudden wrenches of the California culture. The Spanish mission system was challenged by Spanish-Mexican settleres—two generations of whom had by now grown up in California. These were the *Californios*. Because the land was held under the mission system, the *Californios* could not own property. When Mexico declared its independence from Spain in 1821, another cultural jolt was in store for all of those in California. The cry arose for secularization of the missions as the only way to open land to private ownership. In 1830, only twenty-one parcels of land were in private hands. The order came in 1833, and over the next sixteen years the mission ranches were parceled out by the government of Mexico to political favorites.

Greedy land settlers moved in from both the United States and Mexico. The Indians suffered. Through each era, like tragic children, sometimes angry and cruel, the first Californians seemed to come out last.

Evangelization and slavery had been conveniently merged and prosperity had grown startingly by the eve of the breakup of the missions. More than 30,000 Christian Indians tilled the soil under the direction of sixty padres and three hundred soldiers at twenty-one missions. They herded 396,000 head of cattle, 62,000 horses, 321,000 hogs, sheep and goats, and harvested 123,000 bushels of grain in one year. If in no other way, the record of the Franciscans was extraordinary: sixty-five years earlier, there had been in all of California no grain of wheat, no cow, horse, hog, sheep, or goat. But not many years were to pass before the chapel that Serra built at Carmel was to be used for hay storage, and pigs were to be quartered within the San Fernando mission. Not until after 1900 did the missions, by then in crumbling ruins, draw the attention of enough Americans to bring about their restoration as antiquities.

In 1846 came the official end of Mission San Diego de Alcalá. Unable even to support a parish priest, the mission and more than fifty-eight thousand acres of land were granted by Mexican Governor Pio Pico to a government favorite, Don Santiago Arguello. But by then, the United States and Mexico had gone to war over the issue of Texas, its independence and admission into the Union. And, with more at stake than Texas, the war spread quickly to the West Coast.

By 1846, the population of San Diego had grown to only about three-hundred-fifty whites—natives and foreign born—who lived in the area now called Old Town, at the foot of the presidio. As the only important port in Southern California, the town was of obvious strategic value to both the U.S. and Mexico. The town was taken, lost, and taken again by the U.S. forces before the new flag went up to stay.

Many of San Diego's citizens were native Americans who had married Californian women and become Mexican citizens. But with little or no hesitation, they declared their allegiance to the United States. The native population was divided, but the most prominent Spanish families, including the Arguellos, promptly espoused the American cause when they found that war was inevitable. It was clear that Mexico could not hold the country in the face of the growing power of the United States, and they wisely decided to

MEXICAN GOVERNOR Pio Pico with his wife and two nieces during the 1850s. (UT)

throw their influence to the side which could offer personal security, material prosperity, and liberal self-government.

On July 29, 1846, Capt. Samuel F. Dupont arrived from Monterey in the sloop-of-war *Cayne*. With him were John C. Fremont and his company of eighty men, and a like number of Marines; also, Kit Carson, Alexis Godey, and four Delaware Indians. They comprised the California Battalion of volunteers, with Fremont as major. Fremont's orders were to use San Diego as a base for the capture of Los Angeles.

The war in California ended with the battle of San Gabriel, near Los Angeles, on January 9, 1847, just six months later, and the treaty was signed by Fremont for the United States and Andrés Pico for Mexico. From then on, San Diego was undisputed American soil.

Though first in history, San Diego lacked the location and aggressiveness to maintain rank as the metropolis of California. It became a border community with the Treaty of Guadalupe Hidalgo at the close of the Mexican War, when California was ceded to the United States and the international boundary was drawn just south of San Diego.

Gold brought the rush for settlement in Northern California; in the south it was land speculation. But growth did not come so swiftly nor build so solidly as in the north. By the end of the Civil War in 1865, after several years of drought which left Southern California rangeland sere and cattle dying under the sun, fewer than two hundred people lived in the community at the base of the old San Diego Presidio.

"I would not give you five dollars for a deed to the whole of it," cried Alonzo Erastus Horton, a settler from Wisconsin, in 1867. "I would not take it as a gift. It doesn't lie right. Never in the world can you have a city here."

Horton proposed instead to build the city three miles to the south, the site of the present downtown San Diego. He bought 960 acres at an average price of 27 1/2 cents an acre, and left for his adopted home in San Francisco to establish a San Diego land sales office, proclaiming San Diego as the city of the future. It was a minority opinion.

[15]

The rivalry between San Diego and Los Angeles began early. Before the Civil War had ended, Rufus K. Porter reported in the San Francisco *Bulletin*: "The Los Angeles folks do not look with favor at anything tending to promote the prosperity of (San Diego)." David M. Berry, who later helped establish Pasadena, was appalled by San Diego. "The people are all in the real estate business," he wrote, "and will not dig wells and irrigate the land and develop the country ... even the ice they use is made in a factory in Los Angeles...."

Los Angeles began to pull ahead of San Diego in the 1870s, providing the Southern Pacific with a site for a rail depot and a $600,000 grant to bring its lines into Los Angeles from the north and east. Until then it had been assumed that San Diego would be the regional hub. After abortive efforts to make San Diego a transcontinental rail terminus, its citizens settled for a spur line from Los Angeles. A railroad over the precipitous mountains east of San Diego was finally completed in 1919, too late to challenge Los Angeles' supremacy as a transport center. By then Los Angeles had created a man-made harbor, overcoming its handicap in maritime commerce.

Yet there was no easing of hostility between the two Southern California cities. In a special edition after the turn of the century, the *Los Angeles Times* presented a map of the region on which San Diego did not appear. Los Angeles had been moved twenty miles westward on the map (before it finally did indeed annex its way to the Pacific shore) and shown as a port city. San Diego harbor commissioners retaliated with a sketch of San Diego Bay showing 174 nonexistent piers, all busy with traffic between railheads which had not been built, and Pacific shipping lines which in fact did not stop at San Diego.

San Diegans tried futilely to emulate Los Angeles in development of transport and industry. But it was the military that slowly and irrevocably shaped the San Diego future. With World War I, San Diego emerged as a naval bastion offering clear weather for flying, and a deep-water harbor. Those who believed the future of San Diego lay in development of its harbor as a world port proved to be only half right; it was the Navy which grew to provide the bulk of its maritime commerce.

Tourism prospered. Resorts in the suburbs of Coronado and La Jolla grew popular. The Mexican border town of Tijuana became a major tourist attraction during Prohibition, operating wide-open with such blatant lures as "the longest bar in the world." Until a ban on Mexican gambling in 1935, Agua Caliente, a luxurious casino built at a cost of ten million dollars, catered to the film colony and other free spenders of the era. In its day, the high-life of Southern California swirled as much around Agua Caliente as it does today around Las Vegas.

Most of all, two San Diego expositions—in 1915-16 and 1935-36—brought hundreds of thousands of visitors, and some of them never left. The expositions also established a superb architectural nucleus in 1400-acre Balboa Park with the neo-Spanish buildings of the architect Bertram Goodhue; many of them today house galleries, theaters, and museums that are at the cultural heart of the city.

Charles A. Lindbergh had come to San Diego in 1927 to supervise the construction of his *Spirit of St. Louis*, and the city soon developed a stake in the burgeoning aircraft industry. Reuben Fleet, the president of Consolidated Aircraft Corporation at Buffalo, New York, made a decision that was pivotal in San Diego's later emergence as an aero-

THE SAN DIEGO MISSION. From an 1855
sketch by Charles C. Churchill. (TI)

DIEGUENO INDIANS in 1850, after the
Spanish mission system brought civilization
to San Diego's natives: The photograph is from
a stone etching by an artist with the American
Boundary Expedition. (Copley Books)

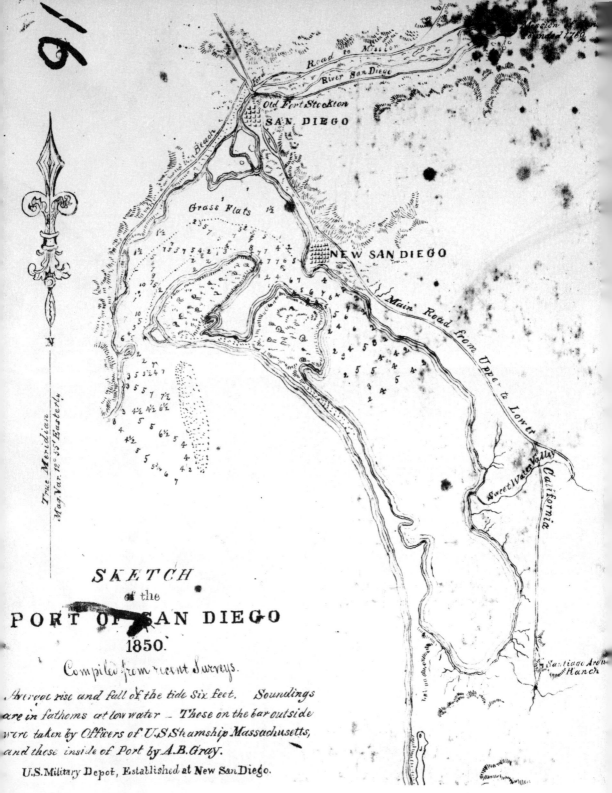

THE PORT OF SAN DIEGO in 1850, after completion of the National Boundary Survey between the United States and Mexico. The sketch was compiled from surveys conducted, in part, by Andrew Gray, the first man to attempt to found a city at New Town. (TI)

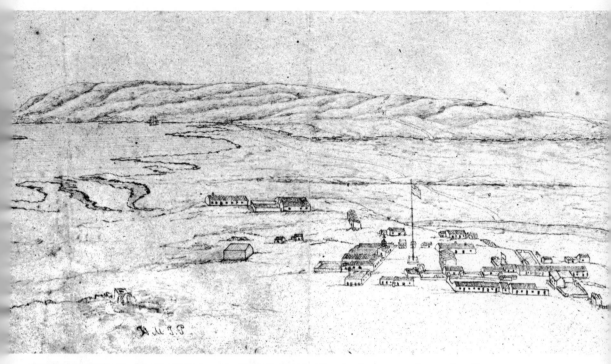

OLD SAN DIEGO, sketched in 1850 by artist H. M. T. Powell: The sketch was one of many Powell made of Old Town, and was the property of the surveyor Andrew B. Gray. (TI)

space center. With a contract to build flying boats for the Navy, Fleet was hampered at Buffalo by icy waters and stormy skies. He moved his factory equipment and his employes to San Diego in special trains. His firm became the foundation for Convair and subsequent divisions of General Dynamics Corporation at San Diego.

In the years since World War II, San Diego has found its civic niche. For years San Diego was divided in a battle of "smokestacks versus geraniums." Some fought for industrial development while others—the geranium faction—strove to maintain San Diego as a placid residential and retirement city.

In the end, the issue was compromised; San Diego, in the 1970s, drew national attention for its success in directing and controlling the nature of its growth.

ALONZO ERASTUS HORTON as a young man. (TI)

ALONZO HORTON and his second wife, Sarah Wilson Babe. (TI)

Alonzo Horton's New Town: 1870 to 1900

SAN DIEGO celebrated its bicentennial in 1969, seven years ahead of the nation's two-hundredth birthday. San Diego's beginnings trace to Junípero Serra, and the founding of his first mission in California at San Diego in 1769.

But the metropolis that has become San Diego—by 1976 the ninth largest city in the United States—has its beginnings with the man named Alonzo Horton.

Alonzo Erastus Horton was born of Puritan stock, the descendant of impoverished English ancestors who came to America in the early seventeenth century. One of seven children of Erastus and Tryphena Burleigh Horton, he was born in Union, Connecticut, on October 24, 1813. While he was still very young, his family moved to Oswego, a village on Lake Ontario in upstate New York.

As a young man, Horton labored as a lumberjack and grocer. By his twenty-first birthday, he had saved enough to buy a small boat, which he used to trade wheat between Oswego and Canada. But his first business enterprise was short-lived. When he was twenty-two, doctors advised him that the cause of a plaguing cough was consumption, and urged him to leave New York State and go West.

West, in 1836, was Wisconsin, and from that year until 1851, Horton traded cattle, speculated in land, and grew wealthy and restive. He had married in 1841, but his wife died five years later, a victim of the same disease which had driven Horton to Wisconsin.

During those fifteen years he spent in Wisconsin, Horton built his first city, Hortonville. It was growing and prospering in 1850 when he received enthusiastic letters from two brothers who had joined the Gold Rush to California. The lure of new frontiers and new fortunes grew irresistible to Horton. In 1851, two years short of his fortieth birthday, he sold Hortonville for $7000 and set out on the long sea journey to California.

First, Horton invested in a mining company, but when that failed, he went into the fields himself. The gold fields, too, were a disappointment. By then, most of the easily found gold had been taken. Horton gave up and returned to more familiar means of making a living. He opened a store in the little mining town of Pilot Hill in El Dorado County, brought water to the settlement, sold ice, and bought and sold gold dust from the mines.

The gold dust speculation turned a healthy profit, netting him as much as $1000 a month, so that by 1854, he had accumulated adequate wealth and sufficient adventure to plan a return to Wisconsin. He boarded the steamer *Cortez* for Panama, where passengers were required to leave one ship, cross the Isthmus by land, and board another ship to complete the voyage.

While the passengers from the *Cortez* were crossing Panama, a native riot erupted, and Horton and the others were caught in the middle. They were dining in a hotel when the natives stormed it. They fled upstairs and Horton, grabbing one loaded pistol after another, held off the mob. After several natives had been slain, the mob retreated, and Horton led the other passengers back to the ship.

Horton returned to Wisconsin, where he remained for several years, taking a second wife, Sarah Wilson Babe. But in 1862, with the memory of California still ripe, he returned to the Pacific Coast.

After a failure in the real estate business, and an abortive attempt at a mining operation in British Columbia, he went into the furniture business in San Francisco.

It did not last long. At the age of fifty-four, Alonzo Horton was still a restless young man. By instinct and training, he was a trader and shrewd speculator, and the quiet life of a furniture dealer ran against the grain. Horton attended a lecture in San Francisco on the ports of California, and the prospects of San Diego. He began to dream. In an interview in 1905, he told of his decision to abandon his furniture business and move to San Diego:

"I could not sleep that night for thinking about San Diego, and at two o'clock in the morning I got up and looked on a map to see where San Diego was, and then went back to bed satisfied. In the morning, I said to my wife: 'I am going to sell my goods and go to San Diego and build a city.' She said I talked like a wild man, that I could not dispose of my goods in six months. But I commenced that morning and made a large sale that day . . .. By the end of the third day I had five men hired and in three days I had sold out all my stock. My wife said she would not oppose me any longer, for she had always noticed when it was right for me to do anything, it always went right in my favor; and as this had gone that way, she believed it was right for me to do so."

Horton booked passage on a steamer, and on April 15 was carried ashore from the ship in San Diego Bay by an Indian, near what is now the foot of Market Street. He later wrote:

"We had to wait there an hour for a wagon to come and take us up to San Diego. While we were waiting, I walked up to where the courthouse now is and looked over the ground. There was nothing there but sagebrush then. I thought San Diego must be heaven-on-earth, if it was as fine as that; it seemed to me the best spot for building a city I ever saw."

He was not the first to envision a city where downtown San Diego lies today. Before the National Boundary Survey between the United States and Mexico was completed in

THE FIRST RESIDENCE in Andrew Gray's New San Diego belonged to Gray's partner, the wealthy San Franciscan William Heath Davis. (TI)

1849, one of the commission, a surveyor Andrew Gray, had camped at the spot where Alonzo Horton stepped ashore eighteen years later and was enthusiastic about the prospects for a new city.

He was introduced to William Heath Davis, a San Francisco businessman who had married into an old San Diego family. Though Davis remained a San Francisco resident, he visited San Diego often. It was on one of these visits that Gray and Davis met. They talked at length about the possibility of building a city, and Gray's enthusiasm infected the wealthy Davis.

The men formed a partnership and bought 160 acres of land from city trustees for $2304. Davis built a wharf out into the bay from the foot of Market Street, and the U.S. Government built a supply house and store at the end of the wharf. Gray and Davis convinced a government official in San Diego to secure defenses on the Indian and Mexican frontier, and to build new barracks in the new town. The official, not surprisingly, became an immediate partner in the new city.

Davis bought a shipment of prefabricated houses from Portland, Maine, and by the end of 1850 there were several homes, two hotels, a lumber yard, and three stores in the new town.

But late the following year, a fire in San Francisco nearly wiped out Davis' empire. His estimated losses were seven hundred thousand dollars. Money for building a city evaporated, and by 1852 the struggling new town gave up. The government barracks remained, but even they were lost in a flood in 1862. Davis' wharf was demolished for firewood by the stranded troops. When Horton arrived in 1867, the new town, known by then as "Davis' Folly," was barren.

After an hour-long ride across the empty land, Horton found himself in Old Town. He was appalled. An agent of Wells Fargo & Company, who had accompanied him on the steamer from San Francisco, and who had extolled the virtues of San Diego, asked Horton what he thought. "I would not give you five dollars for a deed to the whole of it," Horton snapped.

[23]

Ephraim Morse, one of the first Americans to settle in Old Town, and one of the city's most successful merchants, overheard Horton's derision, and asked Horton where he thought the city should lie.

"Right down there by the wharf," Horton said. "I have been nearly all over the United States, and that is the prettiest place for a city I ever saw."

Horton was ready to buy, but the town was not ready to sell the land. Eager, but not ready. San Diego was governed by a board of trustees with limited powers and responsibility to the State Legislature. There had been no election in San Diego for more than two years, and the legal authority to dispose of the lands was in question. Horton approached the county clerk, George Pendleton, and with the offer of ten dollars to cover costs, Pendleton was persuaded to prepare for a new election of trustees.

On the following Sunday, Horton attended services at the town's Catholic chapel, conspicuously depositing a five dollar role of silver coins in the collection plate. The offering drew the attention of the priest, Antonio Ubach, who after the service asked Horton his business.

Horton said he intended to found a new city at San Diego, but was awaiting the election of trustees so he could purchase the land. Father Ubach asked whom Horton desired as trustees, and Horton could name just one man, Ephraim Morse. Ubach suggested Joseph Mannasse and Thomas Bush as the other two.

The election was held on April 27, 1867, with Morse, Mannasse, and Bush chosen unanimously.

The three immediately adopted a resolution for the sale "of certain farming lands." The sale was conducted on May 10, and Horton purchased 960 acres, in 160-acre lots, for $265. The average price was 27 1/2 cents an acre.

Horton's next problem consisted of finding buyers. He returned to San Francisco and opened a land sales office.

FATHER ANTONIO UBACH, pastor of the tiny Catholic Church in Old Town, was a native of Spain who had been ordained in San Francisco and had come to San Diego in 1866. Father Ubach became the protector of San Diego's displaced Indians in the tradition of Junipero Serra and the Franciscan missionaries, baptizing their children, administering last rites, and visiting their encampments in San Diego's back country. (TI)

THE CITY of San Diego at Old Town, when Alonzo Horton arrived in 1867. (TI)

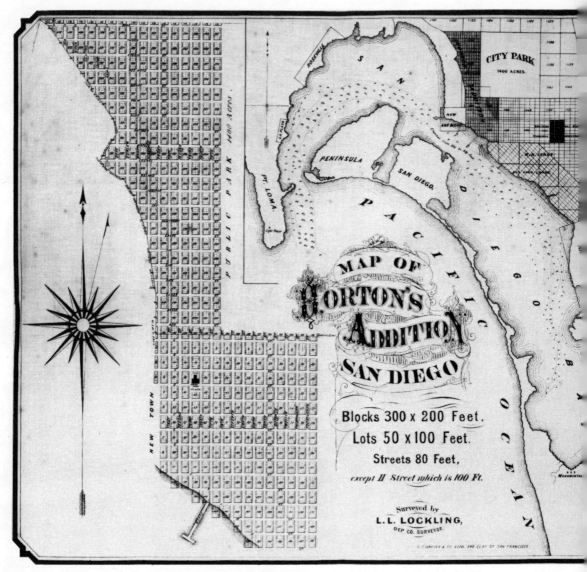

THE LEGAL MAP of Horton's Addition, surveyed by L. L. Lockling in 1867. (TI)

[26]

THE EMBRYONIC CITY of New San Diego—Horton's Addition—just three years after Alonzo Horton's arrival: By 1870, when this, the first available photograph of New Town, was taken. Horton and his agents were selling up to a thousand dollars worth of lots a day. (TI)

AMONG THE FIRST business buildings erected in New Town was this two-story brick edifice on Sixth Avenue and J Street. It was Horton's office for a time, then in 1870 became San Diego's first bank. A group of businessmen raised $100,000 to open the bank, and elected Horton its president. But Horton, who kept his fortunes in a San Francisco bank, soon resigned. He was, he said, taking in more money from his real estate sales than the bank acquired from all its depositors. (TI)

BY THE SUMMER of 1870, the city's major newspaper, *The San Diego Union,* which had scorned Horton's Addition, began to adopt a more friendly attitude. (The fact that Horton had canceled his advertising with the paper, and promised to renew it only if *The Union* would join him in New Town, surely helped in the decision.) The tide was turning away from Old Town, and *The Union* rode the waves. The newspaper's first building in New Town was this two-story frame structure at Fourth Avenue and D Street (later Broadway). (TI)

[27]

THE TRUMP in Alonzo Horton's bid to make New Town the unchallenged center of San Diego was his Horton House, on D Street, between Third and Fourth avenues. It was completed in October 1870 at a cost of $150,000. The hotel boasted heated rooms, hot and cold running water, and lavish furnishings that placed it among the finest hotels on the West Coast. Horton nearly went bankrupt during the ambitious construction project, and managed to secure furnishings on a time-payment plan, almost unheard of in that day. The first clerk at Horton House was a twenty-year-old man by the name of George W. Marston, who would become one of New Town's most successful merchants and greatest supporters. (TI)

HORTON'S HALL, at Sixth and F, was also completed in 1870. The lower level was used as a dry goods store, and the upstairs doubled as a theater and meeting hall. The theater seated up to four hundred, and at one time was a church to both the Presbyterians and Catholics. (TI)

IN 1870, PROPERTY in New Town was assessed at $2.3 million, and the population had reached a staggering 2,301. The town was becoming a city. Mindful of the shift to New Town, the County Board of Supervisors voted to move the county seat to Horton's Addition, outraging Old Town diehards. A local judge fired three board members and stacked a new board, which then blocked removal of county records from Old Town. The issue finally was resolved in the State Supreme Court. The court decided in favor of the original board and New Town. Supervisors moved into temporary quarters at Sixth and G until the erection of the new County Courthouse, shown in this 1872 photograph (upper right) nearing completion at Front and D. (TI)

[29]

BUSINESS CONDITIONS in San Diego fluctuated between boom and bust, depending on news of a railroad for the new city. And the news, in 1872, that San Diego was to become the western terminus for the Texas & Pacific sparked a wildfire of speculation and building. In the two months following the news, Horton sold $83,000 in lots and announced plans for a $45,000 bank block at the corner of Third and D. Offices within the building were to be used by the Texas & Pacific. But the boom went bust shortly after completion of the bank block. The stock market collapsed, and attempts to sell bonds to finance the railroad went for naught. In a few months, the city's population dropped from 5,000 to less than 1,500, and Horton took a financial whipping. (TI)

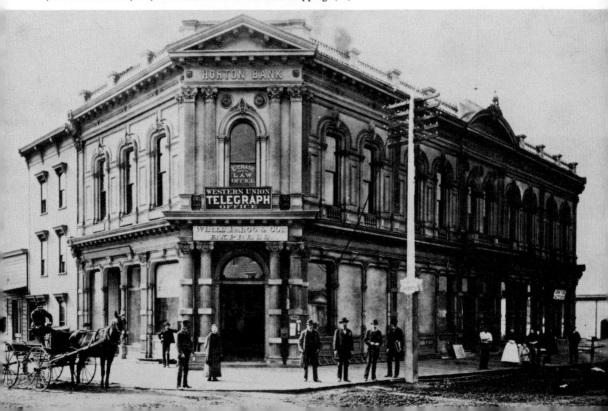

THE THRIVING METROPOLIS of 1874, looking north on Fifth Avenue from Market Street, the town's center. (TI)

GEORGE MARSTON had stayed on as a clerk at Horton House just long enough to get to know the new town. After clerking for Joseph Nash, Marston and a partner, Charles Hamilton, bought him out. In 1878, Marston opened his own dry goods store on Fifth and D, but later that year moved to this site at Fifth and F. Offices upstairs were occupied by a dentist and civil engineer. (TI)

THE BUST of the 1870s left time for the pursuit of leisure. This baseball field, bounded by Sixth, Seventh, C and D, was owned by L. L. Lockling. Horton had given the block to Lockling in payment for his services in surveying and mapping Horton's Addition. San Diego fielded two teams, the Young Americans and the Golden Eagles, who competed against each other, and a team from Old Town. The uniform of the day: boiled shirt and starched bosom. (TI)

THE BOOM OF THE SEVENTIES would be little more than a pop when compared with the explosive 1880s. Frank Kimball, the major proprietor of National City, a few miles south of New Town, went to Boston in 1880 to plead San Diego's case for a railroad. The news that followed him to Boston was bleak: "The people are leaving every day and soon all will be gone who can get away." Kimball persuaded the Santa Fe-Atlantic & Pacific Railroad to establish its West Coast terminus at National City on San Diego Bay. The railroad was to run north from National City to San Diego, then on to Barstow and the East. In the early 1880s, San Diegans gathered regularly at Horton Plaza, eagerly receiving word of new developments in the coming of the railroad. (TI)

[31]

SAN DIEGO'S DREAMS of greatness were inextricably tied to its natural harbor, and the harbor boomed with the railroad boom of the eighties. Pacific Coast Steamship Company, at the foot of Fifth Avenue at Horton's Wharf, provided cheap and convenient transportation to and from San Francisco, just two days north by sea. San Diego's port, with the coming of the railroad, was to become the transfer point of trade between the East Coast and the Orient. (TI)

[32]

THE FIRST SPADEFUL of dirt was turned on December 20, 1880, and by July of 1881, the first train made its way north from National City. But it was four years later when the first train left San Diego to join the line east from Bartow. (TI)

DURING THE 1880s, "Father" Horton's influence began to wane. He had lost money and power in the aftermath of the first unsuccessful railroad bid but, during the second boom, Horton's fortunes picked up somewhat. By 1885, he was able to realize his early dream of building a mansion atop a hill. The mansion (located on the block bounded by First, Second, Fir, and Grape) cost Horton $25,000. It was the city's finest home, with twelve large rooms, woodwork of rare, costly redwood, and fireplaces of inlaid marble. (TI)

THE PROMISE of a railroad brought a flood of newcomers. By 1885, San Diego's population was back to 5,000, and with the completion of the railroad, new arrivals were estimated at 2,500 a month. It was impossible to build hotels and homes fast enough to accommodate the masses, and lumber had to be imported by ship to even attempt to meet the housing needs. (TI)

WHEN THE FIRST through train to the East left National City and arrived in San Diego, it pulled up to a makeshift, $300 Santa Fe station at the foot of Broadway. Perhaps the best visible evidence of San Diego's link with the East was the new Grand Union Depot, completed little more than a year later, in 1887. It was built on the site of the original wooden station, on land donated by the city. (TI)

DURING THE HEIGHT of the booming eighties, there were 64 grocery stores and 71 bars, and more prostitutes than grocerymen and saloon keepers together. San Diego was a wide-open town, despite sporadic attempts to clean things up. Marcus Cohen's tailoring shop did a modest business compared to The Hole in the Wall next door, which advertised: "Tom and Jerrys—Day and Night." The Hole was one of scores of bars that lined Fifth Avenue down to the wharf. (TI)

ONE SURE DRAW was a barbecue. Free transportation, free food, and free music, provided by an omnipresent local band, were enough to bring out a healthy mix of freeloaders and prospective land owners. The feast was something less than gourmet, and the would-be men of property often competed with fleas and flies for the day's sustenance *(below)*. (TI)

SAN DIEGO'S HOTELS could accommodate two thousand in 1887, at the height of the real estate boom, and what you see is what late arrivals got—Spartan lodgings in hastily assembled tents. (TI)

SUCH AN ARRANGEMENT today would almost certainly doom both enterprises, but in 1885, undertaker John Young and his neighbors, the butchers Selwyn and Allison, apparently saw nothing amusing in their side-by-side business relationship on Seventeenth Street. (TI)

[36] SAN DIEGO'S MUSSEL BEACH of the early 1880s became Ocean Beach. Despite a journey of several hours by wagon, New Towners flocked to the beach for Sunday school picnics and mussel roasts. In 1886, colorful twenty-two-year-old promoter, and former page in the State Legislature, Billy Carlson, arrived in San Diego; he bought the beach area and changed the name to Ocean Beach. The maiden lot sale drew a thousand prospective buyers in April 1887, and Carlson sold 2,500 lots, at up to $60 each, in one day. (TI)

FOR YEARS AFTER the establishment of Horton's Addition a number of Diegueno Indians remained encamped in the hills close to the city. One was El Capitan, a self-proclaimed chief. He claimed ownership of all the pueblo lands and pressed a demand for a 25-cent handout from any citizen at any time. He somehow managed to find a good-humored judge who composed an official-looking document certifying his claim, and the citizenry, in general, complied with the order until El Capitan's death. (TI)

EVIDENCES OF BIG-CITY status, however subtle, were cause for celebration among San Diegans. In 1886, the city joined other big-league cities in the chartering of an electric light company. Street lighting was provided by a series of 110-foot masts, topped with clusters of arc lamps. This view of booming San Diego was taken from the tower of the Pierce-Morse five-story skyscraper at Sixth and F. (UT)

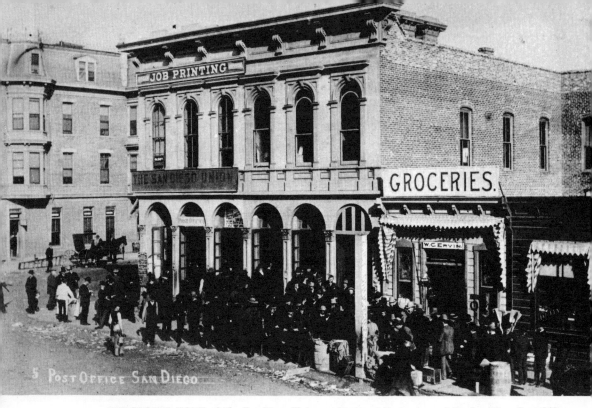

THE SECOND HOME of *The San Diego Union,* at Sixth and F, also housed the San Diego Post Office in 1887. The queues here are probably waiting for mail rather than the morning edition. Two doors down the street was the more modest headquarters of the short-lived *San Diego Bee,* which was bought out by the *Union* the following year. (TI)

THE LION CLOTHIERS at 945 Fifth Avenue then, as now, specialized in gents' furnishings. The three best-dressed gentlemen to the immediate right of the front door are not customers. They're dummies. (TI)

WITH THE FURIOUS land dealing of the boom came title insurance companies to protect against fast dealings. San Diego Title and Abstract Company, which years later evolved into Title Insurance and Trust Company of San Diego, was headed by San Diego Mayor D. C. Reed (far left). (TI)

BY LATE 1887, the boom was in full swing, and it was not unusual for $200,000 worth of real estate to change hands in a single day. Everyone, it seemed, was in the real estate business; and if not real estate, then something related. At this establishment, you could buy a lot or house from a realtor on the boardwalk, and contract to have it painted and wallpapered. (TI)

RAPID TRANSIT, circa 1887: San Diego, surrounded by subdivisions, boasted something even cosmopolitan San Francisco could not claim: electric rail cars. The line, when working, ran from the Pacific Coast Steamship Company's wharf to University Heights. (TI)

THE FAMED MARSHALL of the Western Plains, Wyatt Earp *(left),* was attracted by reports of a boom sweeping Southern California. By then, Earp had seen enough of Dodge City and Arizona (he was, in fact, under indictment in Arizona for shooting men who had slain his brother). Earp arrived in San Diego in 1887 *(below)* and took residence in the Schmidt Block (left) on Third Avenue, opposite Horton Plaza. He set up three gambling establishments: one there, one on Sixth, and another on E Street. Gambling was legal, and Earp was one of San Diego's most respected citizens. He was listed in the San Diego City Directory for 1889 as a "Capitalist." He refereed boxing matches as a sideline to raising capital at his gambling dens. (UT)

ONE OF SAN DIEGO'S four baseball teams, Schiller & Murtha, in 1887: By the booming eighties, the teams that played at the Lockling Block had graduated from starched collars to baseball uniforms. (TI)

AT THE HEIGHT of the boom, the two men who were to become San Diego's premier promoters arrived on the scene, Elisha S. Babcock and H. L. Story. They came to San Diego from the Midwest, as had so many others, seeking to recover their health. While hunting rabbits on Coronado Island, Babcock and Story discussed plans to develop the island and build a resort hotel to attract buyers. They purchased all of Coronado and North Island in December 1885, for $110,000, and incorporated the Coronado Beach Company. Babcock and Story quickly peddled more than $1,000,000 worth of lots. In this 1886 photo *(above)*, Babcock (right in group of three) and Story (left) survey the Coronado shoreline with Alonzo Horton (hat and cane). Babcock and Story organized the San Diego and Coronado Ferry Company in 1886 *(below)* to ply prospective buyers from the foot of Market Street across the bay to Coronado. (TI)

[41]

ARCHITECTS James and Merritt Reid were given free rein by Babcock and Story, and the new Hotel del Coronado, mostly built with unskilled labor, became the best advertised property in the United States. As if construction of the most expensive hotel on the West Coast were not enough to attract attention, the promoters conjured up all manner of gimmicks to draw the curious to Coronado. In 1887, with completion of Hotel del Coronado at the half-way point, thousands of San Diegans and tourists gathered *(below)* to watch the ascension of the *City of Tia Juana* hot-air balloon. (TI)

THE FINISHED PRODUCT, the Hotel del Coronado, built at a cost of more than one million dollars. (TI)

WATER WAS SOMETHING San Diegans fought for and worried over from the beginning. In the early days of New Town, residents sank small wells, or purchased water that had been carried from the San Diego River. It was enough for a small town with little prospect of outgrowing its supply. But by the 1880s, it was clear that the city's snowballing population would soon demand more. In the mid-eighties, T. S. Van Dyke and W. E. Robinson formed a million-dollar corporation to dam waters on Boulder Creek in the Cuyamaca Mountains, fifty miles to the east. They constructed a 45-mile flume to carry the water across canyons on 315 trestles and through eight tunnels to pipes in the city. It was completed in February of 1889. There was to be a celebration when the first water reached San Diego, but failure to provide valves in some sections of pipe left them air-locked, and reduced the flow to a trickle. Not to miss a celebration, the builders diverted some San Diego River water into the pipes until the problem was corrected. The unknowing revelers were ecstatic over the purity of the "mountain" water. Sharing a front-row seat for a staged ride on the flume are California Governor Robert Waterman (right) and San Diego Mayor D. C. Reed. (TI)

[43]

AMONG THE MOST ambitious water-saving projects of the day was the Sweetwater Dam, built in 1887 to assure a water supply for the development of the South Bay area. Two of the men who helped promote construction of the dam were Frank Kimball (right) the developer of National City, and W. G. Dickinson. (TI)

DRILLING FOR WATER on Point Loma in 1885. (TI)

A CULTURAL MIGRATION of sorts occurred during the boom of the 1880s, and one of the more colorful immigrants was Benjamin Henry Jesse Shepard *(left)*, a tall, esthetic bachelor with a handlebar moustache, who came to San Diego at the age of thirty-eight. A musician and spiritualist, Shepard had studied literature under Alexander Dumas, and became a concert pianist, he said, without a lesson. He was immediately adopted by San Diego's culture-starved, who supplied the funds with which he built his Villa Montezuma *(below)*, a showplace of stained-glass windows and rich woods. Shepard claimed the home was being built under the direction of the spirits. He held occasional concerts and seances there, but with the collapse of the boom, Shepard headed for Los Angeles and greener cultural pastures. (TI)

[44]

FRANK TERRILL BOTSFORD set up shop in 1887 and began surveying the land that would one day become San Diego's most valuable residential property: La Jolla. Botsford subdivided much of the land around La Jolla Park, which he developed, and began selling lots at public auction in the late 1880s. (TI)

SAN DIEGO'S population had reached 35,000 by 1888. The streets and saloons were crowded, and hotels and rooming houses were full. But the bubble was about to burst. San Diego had its railroad, but it was never more than a spur line. Business in San Diego had increased, and the quiet years seemed over. But the wharfs and warehouses had not filled with the goods of the world. The big cargo ships never came, and the Santa Fe had pushed on to Los Angeles. San Diego's boom had fed on itself, and there was little industry or trade to support the thousands of newcomers. Not everyone could sell real estate forever. But some tried. (TI)

[45]

THE CRASH HAD COME by April of 1888. Faster by far than they had come, people began to leave. Within six months the population was reduced by more than half, to 16,000. Those who were left found themselves holding inflated property which the speculators had unloaded at the first sign of trouble. More than $2 million was withdrawn from the city's eight banks. Los Angeles had won, without a doubt. San Diego's 1890 population was 16, 159. Los Angeles' population: 50,000 in the city, and more than 100,000 in the county. (TI)

"SUGAR PRINCE" John D. Spreckels arrived in San Diego a few months before the crash of 1888. And when it seemed that everyone would flee the dying city, Spreckels brought his millions to stay. The heir to the Spreckels sugar fortunes discovered San Diego quite by accident. He was on a pleasure cruise along the California coast when his yacht *Lurline* ran short of supplies and sailed into San Diego Bay. The city formed a delegation to greet the distinguished visitor, and, though he was not to become a permanent resident for another fifteen years, Spreckels fell victim to the San Diego hard-sell. (UT)

AMONG SPRECKELS' first investments in San Diego were the wharf and coal bunkers at the foot of G Street. The Santa Fe Railroad had talked of abandoning San Diego because of poor facilities and the unavailability of coal. But once Spreckels built the wharf and bunkers (for $90,000), tracks were laid between the railroad and the wharf. The Santa Fe stayed and Spreckels was a local hero. (TI)

PRESIDENT BENJAMIN HARRISON visited San Diego on April 23, 1891, during a tour of the West Coast. The president and his wife were taken on a parade through the city and past the home of staunch Republican Alonzo Horton. The parade ended at Horton Plaza with a massive rally of 5,000 San Diegans. Harrison, the first U.S. president to visit San Diego, told the crowd: "If there were no other reward for our journey across the continent, what we have seen here today about your harbor would have repaid us for all the toll of travel." (TI)

[47]

DURING HIS VISIT, President Harrison (center, descending steps) toured the Hotel del Coronado, which by then was deeply in debt. Babcock and Story were threatened with foreclosure and only a $100,000 loan from Spreckels kept the hotel alive. (TI)

CABLE CARS came to San Diego in 1890, as they came to Los Angeles and San Francisco. But they lasted only a short time. The line ran from the southwest corner of Fourth Avenue and Spruce Street, past the Florence Hotel, to C Street, then from C to Sixth, and down to the waterfront. The cable cars stopped dead in March 1892, when the San Diego Cable Railroad was declared insolvent. (TI)

THE FIRST NATIONAL BANK was one of the survivors of the bust. But there were spectacular failures. Among the most notable of the era was the California National Bank. The bank was organized in 1888 by two adopted San Diegans, D. D. Dare and J. W. Collins. The bank was considered sound until 1891, when suddenly, in October, a sign went up on the door: "Closed Temporarily." Lost in the shuffle were $200,000 and D. D. Dare, who reportedly had fled to Europe. Not as fast, Collins was apprehended, charged with embezzlement, and held under guard at the Brewster Hotel. While waiting to be taken to Los Angeles and jailed, Collins walked into the bathroom and fired one shot into the air. Friends came and quickly removed him in a casket. It was reported later that Collins had joined his former partner in Europe. (TI)

TO COMMEMORATE Cabrillo's landing, 350 years earlier, San Diegans turned out en masse on September 28, 1892. Three days of festivities were planned, the first of which was to include a reenactment of Juan Rodriguez Cabrillo's landing. But technical problems caused long delays, and by the time the *San Salvador* and Cabrillo were ready to land, the tide had gone out. Cabrillo and his ship were stranded in mud, 300 feet from shore. (TI)

THE LITTLE LADY at left was one of the Luiseno Indians who lived around San Diego. She was brought to the city for the first Cabrillo celebration in 1892. Her claim to be 128 years old seems unlikely. On the other hand . . . (TI)

FATHER UBACH brought in a group of Indians from San Luis Rey for the celebration, and staged an Indian Fiesta. A stockade was built on the block bounded by A, Ash, Third, and Fourth, and the Indians danced in costumes of paint and feathers. (TI)

THE FISHER OPERA HOUSE was a major contribution to San Diego's cultural scene in the 1890s. Built by John C. Fisher, the opera house cost more than $100,000 and was called one of the best theatres in the West. The Fisher Opera House was financed with money loaned by the California National Bank, and was forced into receivership when the bank failed. It later became Madame Katherine Tingley's Isis Theatre, and still later, a movie house. (TI)

WHILE ON THE WEST COAST visiting a sister near Los Angeles, E. W. Scripps *(left)*, the newspaper tycoon, made a weekend trip to San Diego in 1890. Scripps, who was not yet forty, was considering retirement, and although his first impressions of San Diego were of a busted boom town, the city appealed to him. It was, he said, "3,000 miles from the people who bothered me about my newspaper and their own political or business ambitions." Scripps laid out his Miramar Ranch *(below)* on 400 acres about sixteen miles north of the city. He was officially retired, but it was not long before he was back in the newspaper business, advancing the money to Paul Blades and E. E. Hickman to buy the *San Diego Sun.* (TI)

BILLY CARLSON, the young man who had developed Ocean Beach during the boom of the eighties, was the winning candidate for mayor of San Diego in 1892. A mere twenty-nine years old, he was soon dubbed San Diego's "Boy Mayor." Carlson had two opponents in the race, one of whom was Capt. James E. Friend. Friend thought he had lots of friends. His nominating petition was signed by 1,100, but he received a meager ninety-eight votes. Friend later wrote a book about the episode which he titled *One Thousand Liars.* Carlson was reelected in 1894, but after losing his bid for reelection again in 1896, he moved on to Los Angeles, but something went wrong. Carlson was next heard from as a resident of San Quentin. He was last heard from during the 1930s, when he wrote to the City Council applying for a job as San Diego's city manager. (TI)

THE LAST SPIKE of the rail line connecting San Diego with La Jolla was driven on May 15, 1894. San Diego was recovering some of its confidence by the mid-1890s, and developers began to regain some of their courage. The San Diego, Old Town and Pacific Beach Line, that had passed into the hands of Spreckels, was extended to La Jolla, which was languishing without transportation. The rail line later was converted to electricity. (TI)

[51]

GOLD COUNTRY San Diego was not, but the extension of the San Diego, Cuyamaca and Eastern Railroad, as far as Foster, brought renewed mining activity for a time. The Stonewall Mine at Lake Cuyamaca was one of the few successful mining ventures. Discovered in 1870 by pioneer prospector James Skidmore, the mine reportedly yielded $300,000 worth of gold in its first three years. It was originally named the Stonewall Jackson Mine, but strong sentiment among some of the migrant Rebels in the area soon led to the dropping of the last name. For a time, Governor Waterman had been a principal owner. But by 1893, after having given up about $2,000,000 in gold, the mine closed down. (TI)

THOUGH COMPLETED in 1888, the La Jolla Park Hotel did not open until 1893, following completion of the rail line to La Jolla. Situated on Prospect Street at the end of Girard Avenue, the hotel was advertised as competition for Hotel del Coronado. It came in a poor second. Closed in 1896, the La Jolla Park Hotel burned shortly thereafter. It was heavily insured, as were many other San Diego resort hotels that failed in the eighties and nineties and somehow, later, caught fire. (TI)

[52]

SAN DIEGO'S FINEST in 1890 . . . (TI)

. . . AND IN 1899. The policemen worked twelve hours a day and earned $100 a month, with no days off, until 1895. Then hours were cut to eight a day, and pay was cut to $75 a month. Mounted policemen were allowed an extra $25 a month for care and feed of their horses. (UT)

THE BAR SCENE in the Gay Nineties: The sign on the wall behind the bartender at left is a gentle reminder: "Don't Forget the Bottle for Sunday." (TI)

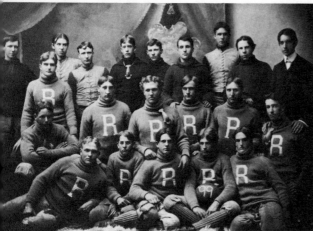

RUSS HIGH SCHOOL football heroes in 1899. (TI)

SAN DIEGO COUNTRY CLUB, the city's first golf club, was organized in 1897. The University Heights Land Company donated acreage near Upas Street and Park Boulevard. The duffers of the day played on dirt, sand, and weeds. (TI)

THE OLD SPANISH LIGHTHOUSE was, in fact, neither old nor Spanish. It was built by the U.S. Government in 1851, after California had gained statehood. The lighthouse was a popular attraction for tourists and picnickers, though the only route was over a narrow and rocky dirt road. (TI)

REUBEN THE GUIDE was one of the more interesting characters of 1890s San Diego, and one of the city's few visible blacks. Dressed as a Mexican, with large sombrero and serape, Reuben met tourists as they arrived by train or ship and offered half-day excursions in his carriage to Tijuana or the "Old Spanish Lighthouse" on Point Loma. (TI)

CHINESE FISHING JUNKS dotted San Diego Bay during the 1880s and 1890s, and there were constant complaints that the Chinese were fishing with fine nets, illegal in San Diego waters. The Chinese answered the complaints by fishing only at night. The large fish were sold locally; the small ones were dried and exported to San Francisco. (TI)

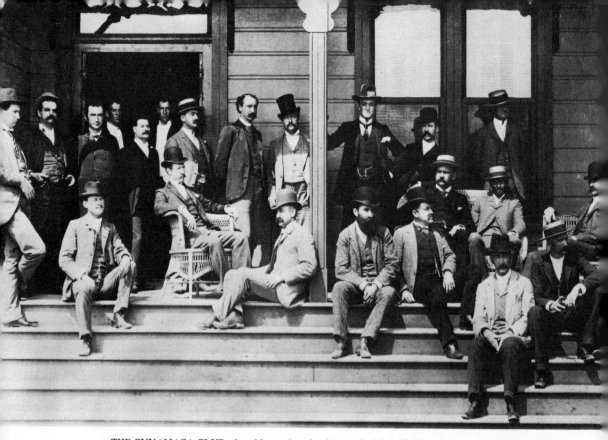

THE CUYAMACA CLUB, the oldest privately chartered club in California, was organized in 1887 as a restricted luncheon club for the men-about-town. Good eating establishments were scarce. In 1899, the club's membership lists were a who's who of San Diego. Members included, from left (on steps), Howard Crittenden, Nat R. Titus, George Fuller, Frank L. Sargent, William L. King, Baker Thomas, and John Monteith; (seated in chairs), W. H. Doud, Patterson Sprigg, M. A. Luce, and Colonel Ensign, (and standing), Oscar Tippett, Howard Kutchin, Daniel Cave, a waiter, William Edwards (the club steward), another waiter, Hampton Story, G. Y. Gray, Watt Reed, Charles Hume, Gaston Miller, and Gus Holterhoff. (TI)

BATHING BEAUTIES of the day, on the beach at Coronado, were in little danger of suffering sunburn. (TI)

SAN DIEGO NORMAL SCHOOL, a state-run college for teachers, was approved by the Legislature in 1897, and classes began the next year when ninety-three students met in rooms at the Hill Block at Sixth and F (the former site of Horton's Hall). Eleven acres in University Heights were set aside for the permanent structures, and the cornerstone was laid in December of 1898. The establishment of San Diego's first college boosted land values in the area east of the city center, and new residential communities sprang up around it. The college was to be a training ground for California teachers, and those who enrolled were required to sign agreements promising to teach upon completion of studies. (TI)

OPENING DAY, San Diego Normal School's first president, Samuel T. Black, said, "No other Normal School had so auspicious an opening," Probably true. Attendance was far less than the ninety-three students enrolled. A circus happened to be in town on the same day. (TI)

EVERYBODY'S DOG, BUM, a Saint Bernard-Spaniel mix, joined the land rush to San Diego in 1887. Much of his story is lost in legend, but some remains in news clips of the day. He arrived aboard a steamer from San Francisco and was adopted by a local Chinese laundryman, Ah Wo Sue. But Bum was no one-man dog. A panhandler from the beginning, he was served the choicest leftovers in local restaurants. His popularity reached such heights in the early 1890s that his picture was printed on all county dog licenses. Bum regularly joined in parades, attended police court, political meetings, and funerals, and came and left by boat or train whenever he yearned to travel. He also frequented the local saloons. Once, while jumping a freight train, Bum lost his right forepaw and a piece of his tail under a wheel. By then, he was already well on the road to alcoholism. The Board of Supervisors, by special order, sent him to the county poor farm to dry out. But damage to his liver, the legend goes, was already too great. He died on November 10, 1898. *The Evening Tribune* ran his obituary: "The death of Bum, that good old dog, will be regretted by all public-spirited citizens. His was a more active life and useful life than nine-tenths of his race." (TI)

HORTON PLAZA, by the 1890s, had become something of a blot on the civic landscape. It had been donated to the city by Alonzo Horton during his flush years as "an attractive place for public meetings, announcements, recreation, or any other public purpose." But by 1890 it had fallen into decay, and Horton, whose finances had diminished equally, offered to sell it to the city if the city would maintain and improve it. City fathers thought they had a bargain. For $10,000, payable at $100 a month, interest free, the park was theirs. And they immediately set about making the desired improvements. Horton was then eighty-one years old, and chances of his living to collect the full $10,00 seemed remote. But the city lost that gamble. Horton had been paid in full by 1903. At eighty-nine, he was still going strong. (TI)

MADISON AVENUE it wasn't—but it was effective advertising in 1898. (TI)

SAN DIEGO CELEBRATES news of the Spanish Intervention Resolution on April 14, 1898. A great procession, led by the City Guard Band, paraded through downtown streets cheering for veterans of the Grand Army of the Republic. A Spanish flag was burned at the *San Diego Union* office, and the crowds cheered President McKinley and Robert E. Lee. (TI)

UNDER THE TRANQUIL surface, turn-of-the-century San Diego is a city about to boom again. (TI)

Growing Up: 1900 to 1920

FOLLOWING THE BOOMING 1880s and the subsequent bust, San Diego had been in a holding pattern.

In 1888, the city's population had peaked at 35,000. A year later it was cut by more than half, to 16,000. And by 1900, it had climbed slowly up to 17,000.

But San Diego was a city that desperately wanted to grow up. Though the people would continue to tie their dreams to railroads and commercial shipping, it would be the military that would irrevocably shape the city's future.

The Spanish-American War had given evidence of San Diego's strategic importance in times of national emergency. And the city's clear flying weather and natural deep-water harbor would attract the military again in World War I.

In the first six years of the new century, San Diego would recover the population it lost in the crash of 1889. John Spreckels, the sugar heir who had invested heavily in San Diego, would remain a San Francisco resident during those six years, and pour millions more of the Spreckels family money into a city he would dominate for the next two decades.

Spreckels already owned the street car system, two of the town's three newspapers, *The San Diego Union* and *Evening Tribune*, most of Coronado and North Island, and Hotel del Coronado, which he had taken over when E. S. Babcock was unable to repay a loan of $100,000.

In 1900, the city's only link with the outside world was the Santa Fe's "Surf Line" running south from Los Angeles. Regardless of the high mountains to the east, or what Los Angeles believed, all railroads into Southern California, San Diegans were convinced, could find a natural terminus at San Diego.

The San Diego-Eastern Railway Committee was formed in 1902, and its incorporators were merchant George Marston, U. S. Grant, Jr., and Babcock. They raised $40,000 by public subscription for engineering studies, and went ahead with their plans. But it would be twenty years before the plans became reality, and it would be Spreckels, in the end, who guaranteed the railroad.

The city had seven miles of paved and 45 miles of graded streets, 15 miles of electric railway, 22 miles of motor railway, 16 miles of cement sidewalks, 25 churches, 14 schools, a $100,000 opera house, and a still-undeveloped 1,400-acre city park in 1900.

Father Alonzo Horton would be on the scene for the next decade, but as leader he would be replaced by men such as Spreckels, Marston, Louis Wilde, D. C. Collier, O. W. Cotton, and Ed Fletcher.

The battle for West Coast supremacy would continue with Los Angeles. In 1901, *The San Diego Union* editorialized:

"The *Los Angeles Times* has just issued a special edition designed to show the resources and development of the county in which it is published. The work as a whole is commendable. Unfortunately, the proprietor of that paper was unable to restrain his chronic hatred of San Diego. So in the map which he publishes, showing the field of Pacific commerce, San Diego is carefully eliminated, and Los Angeles, a city twenty miles in the interior, is moved down the coast and made to appear a port of Southern California, the deception being heightened by various devices representing purely imaginary steamer lines from that fictitious entrepot of commerce."

San Diego's harbor commissioners, in the meantime, issued a report of San Diego's commerce with a sketched bay containing 174 nonexistent piers, all connected to marginal rail lines, and a map of the Pacific Ocean with sea lanes converging at the port of San Diego.

A San Diego Exposition, in 1915-16, would bring hundreds of thousands of visitors, some of whom never left. And San Diego would take a giant step toward its future as a tourist capital.

LYDIA KNAPP HORTON, third wife of Alonzo Horton. (TI)

THE FREE PUBLIC LIBRARY, San Diego's first permanent library facility, was erected in 1902. Lydia Knapp Horton solicited funds for the library from Andrew Carnegie, who was endowing libraries across the country. Mrs. Horton wrote to Carnegie in 1899, outlining San Diego's needs. Her letter brought a prompt reply. "Madam: If the city were to pledge itself to maintain a free public library from taxes . . . I should be glad to give you $50,000 to erect a suitable building." The city provided a site, between Eighth and Ninth streets, and George Marston provided money for landscaping, supervised by Kate Sessions. Carnegie's grant was the first made to a California city. (TI)

THE COMING OF THE AUTO prompted San Diego's established Cycle and Arms Company to expand to the city's first automobile dealership. Bicycles and guns were still the company's mainstay, but for a few dollars more you could purchase a passing fad: the horseless carriage. (TI)

MOVING DAY 1902, when a wealthy physician by the name of Edwards decided to move up to a classier neighborhood in Coronado across the bay. (TI)

OLDEST OF ITS KIND on the West Coast, the San Diego Rowing Club was founded in 1885 and moved to its site on Harbor Drive at the foot of Fifth Avenue, pictured here, in 1900. At one time the club boasted 1,000 members and was twice claimed the Pacific Coast Champions, in 1908 and 1926. (TI)

LA JOLLA'S GREEN DRAGON Colony was established by Anna Held, who came to San Diego with the U. S. Grant, Jr. family in 1894, as governess to the Grant children. She immediately began buying up land in La Jolla, and in the late 1890s and early 1900s started building small cottages on the hillside above Cove Beach. She married singer and musician Max Heinrich and together they laid out the Green Dragon Colony as a cultural center for artists, actors, musicians, and writers. (TI)

LA JOLLA'S COVE BEACH was one of the most popular tourist attractions in turn-of-the-century San Diego. The two cottages (center), still standing in 1976, were built about 1895, and named the "Red Rest" and the "Neptune." (TI)

PROFESSOR HORACE POOLE was one of La Jolla's star attractions. His celebrated high dives from a springboard above the caves near Cove Beach brought weekend throngs. An imitator, Bert Reed, son of the San Diego mayor, attempted a dive from above the caves on August 4, 1898. He missed the rocks below, but was so badly injured that he died three months later. Poole, who received $45 from the railway for each leap, discontinued his dives for a time following Reed's death, but resumed them in the early 1900s. (TI)

TENT CITY, a summer resort on the beach at Coronado, was opened by Spreckels in 1901, and quickly became San Diego's official summer playground. Open streetcars carried guests from the ferry to the end of Tent City. On each side of the tracks were rows of tent cottages, with dirt floors, sparse furnishings, and light provided by a single naked bulb suspended from tent posts. Accommodations may have seemed less than desirable, but it was the "people's resort," in dramatic contrast to the opulent Hotel del Coronado in the background. (UT)

MISSION CLIFF PARK and its exquisite gardens were owned and operated by Spreckels' San Diego Electric Railway Company. While San Diegans debated how best to improve the city's 1,400-acre downtown park, Spreckels brought in landscape architect John Davidson to provide San Diego's citizens with some kind of park facilities. Mission Cliff Park was laid out on the bluffs overlooking Mission Valley at the end of the rail line at Park Boulevard and Adams Avenue. (TI)

THE MISSION CLIFF gardens were landscaped with palm, eucalyptus, cypress, acacia, and cedar trees, and paths were laid out with benches where visitors could look out over Mission Valley below. (TI)

KATHERINE A. TINGLEY, the leader of a group of dissident Theosophists, came to San Diego in 1896, seeking a site for her school to revive the lost mysteries of antiquity. She chose a 130-acre parcel on Point Loma, and in 1898, Madame Tingley and her dissidents opened the Universal Brotherhood & Theosophical Society's international headquarters there. Madame Tingley was known officially as "The Outer Head of the Theosophical Society of America," and unofficially as "The Purple Mother," because of her propensity toward elaborate and flowery purple dresses. (TI)

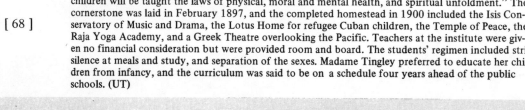

[68]

THE TEMPLE of the Theosophists was described by them as "a temple of living light . . . (where) children will be taught the laws of physical, moral and mental health, and spiritual unfoldment." The cornerstone was laid in February 1897, and the completed homestead in 1900 included the Isis Conservatory of Music and Drama, the Lotus Home for refugee Cuban children, the Temple of Peace, the Raja Yoga Academy, and a Greek Theatre overlooking the Pacific. Teachers at the institute were given no financial consideration but were provided room and board. The students' regimen included strict silence at meals and study, and separation of the sexes. Madame Tingley preferred to educate her children from infancy, and the curriculum was said to be on a schedule four years ahead of the public schools. (UT)

THE MYSTIQUE SURROUNDING the Theosophical Society in the early 1900s gave rise to sensational newspaper accounts accusing Madame Tingley of irregular and dangerous conduct in the handling of impressionable children. The Theosophists' theories of reincarnation drew the wrath of local religious leaders, and Madame Tingley seemed to be constantly entangled in law suits. She won all but one of the suits, including a libel action against the *Los Angeles Times,* which had based a story on reports accusing her of "spookery," starvation of children, and forced-labor practices. She was awarded $7,000. But the suit she lost was eventually her undoing. Madame Tingley was accused by the wife of one of her benefactors of alienating the affections of her husband. Madame Tingley borrowed $400,00 from one of her supporters, the sporting goods magnate A. B. Spalding, part of which was used to cover the judgment against her. But on Spalding's death, his heirs called in the loan, and Madame Tingley was unable to pay. Her death in 1929 left the institute to founder; it finally closed, and the buildings were sold in 1942. (TI)

JOHN L. SEHON, a retired Army captain, was elected mayor in 1905 on the Independent ticket. His opponents, claiming a military pensioner was ineligible for public service, filed suit to bar him from office. To avoid an injunction, Sehon hid out until the eve of the day he was to take office. Guards had been posted in front of the municipal building, so Sehon climbed a ladder to the second floor and broke into the mayor's office. In the morning he was issuing orders. And the suit was dropped. (TI)

OSTRICHES WERE BIG business in San Diego County in the early 1900s. At one time there were 20,000 ostriches being raised in Southern California. One farm, moved from Coronado to Mission Cliff Park, was a popular attraction for tourists. Ostriches were ridden by trainers, and visitors to the park could buy ostrich eggs and plumes for their hats. A San Diego ostrich farmer could make as much as $300 in one day from feathers and eggs. Plumed hats were the rage until 1917, when women were encouraged to abandon luxury items in the war effort. Feathers fell from $350 a pound to $2.50 almost overnight. (TI)

[70]

MIXED DOUBLES on the courts at Hotel del Coronado in 1905, a favorite Southern California pastime. (TI)

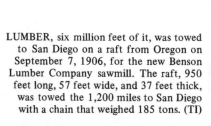

ONE DAY'S CATCH and the proud fisherman at Hotel del Coronado. (TI)

LUMBER, six million feet of it, was towed to San Diego on a raft from Oregon on September 7, 1906, for the new Benson Lumber Company sawmill. The raft, 950 feet long, 57 feet wide, and 37 feet thick, was towed the 1,200 miles to San Diego with a chain that weighed 185 tons. (TI)

THE NAVY GUNBOAT *Bennington* steamed into San Diego Bay on the morning of July 21, 1905, after a stormy trip from Hawaii, and with a crew looking forward to shore leave in San Diego's Stingaree. Instead, they got word from the captain that they would be going to the rescue of the *Wyoming*, which was adrift and in need of a tow to San Francisco. The black gang began furiously pouring coal into the boilers, but a broken gauge failed to register pressure building to the danger point. Valves, which would have allowed any excess pressure to escape, were jammed. In an ugly mood, the gang was downing whiskey as fast as it shoveled coal. Finally, one boiler gave way, slamming into another . . . the subsequent explosion killed 60 of the ship's 197 crewmen and officers. (TI)

Bailey Photo.

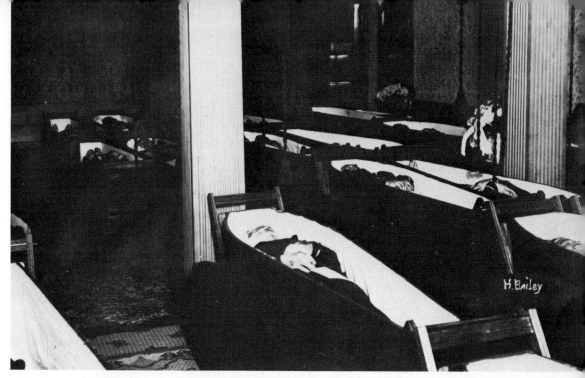

FREIGHT WAGONS and carriages from all over San Diego came to haul the casualties to local mortuaries, and theaters and shops closed in mourning for the victims. (TI)

A MASS BURIAL was held at the national cemetery on Point Loma, attended by practically every Navy man in the city. Father Antonio Ubach presided. The ship was sold at auction, refloated, and served as a molasses barge in the Hawaiian Islands for about fifteen years. (TI)

COPYRIGHT 1905 BY

FATHER ANTONIO UBACH'S funeral on April 3, 1907, drew two thousand mourners to Saint Joseph's Cathedral. Father Ubach had come to San Diego in the 1860s, at a time when many Indians who had known the days of the San Diego Mission still looked to the Church for guidance. Priests from throughout the state participated in the Requiem High Mass, and a line of carriages extending a mile and a half formed the funeral procession to the Catholic cemetery overlooking the bay. (TI)

KEEPING DOWN THE DUST on San Diego's streets provided full-time employment for the watering crews. (TI)

DEL MAR'S STRATFORD INN opened in 1906, and quickly became the "in" place for visiting celebrities. Its 120 luxury rooms were occupied over the years by such filmland notables as Mary Pickford and Douglas Fairbanks, who developed plans for United Artists while staying here. Also signing the guest register were Bing Crosby, Pat O'Brien, Hedda Hopper, Lucille Ball, and Desi Arnaz. The hotel closed in 1964 and was demolished in 1969 after the city council declared the empty relic a public nuisance. (TI)

RENEWED GROWTH, an expanding tourism industry, and a sudden boom in business conditions gave impetus to U. S. Grant, Jr.'s, plans for an elaborate new downtown hotel. Grant *(right)* had taken over Horton House, which by then was thirty-five years old and decaying. The hotel that would replace Horton House would be called the U. S. Grant as a memorial to his father, the former president. Removal of the first brick for demolition of Horton House came on the evening of July 12, 1905. The guest of honor, Alonzo Horton, said he wanted to be the first guest to register at the new hotel. (TI)

BUT THE U. S. GRANT was to be a long time in building. Times were good when Grant conceived the hotel, but a financial crisis and recession that began in the East rolled across the country to California in 1907, and money for construction dried up. All work on the hotel stopped, and the concrete skeleton stood deserted for months. (TI)

NEW MONEY and new life came to San Diego in 1909, and under Louis J. Wilde—now a half-owner of the hotel—the U. S. Grant was finally completed. It opened for its first guests on October 15, 1910, at a final cost of $1,100,000. Furnishings added $250,000. The Grant had two swimming pools, and at the top a grand ballroom called the finest on the West Coast. The Grant, by completion, had become a civic venture. In the end, it was San Diego's citizens, subscribing to the tune of $700,000, who built the hotel. (TI)

THE GREAT WHITE FLEET called at San Diego on April 14, 1908, and the arrival meant to San Diegans that the United States was beginning to take notice of the city which anchored the country's West Coast. The fleet was on an around-the-world cruise under orders from Pres. Theodore Roosevelt, who wanted to impress the world, and particularly Japan, with the U.S. military might. Under command of Rear Adm. R. D. Evans, the fleet consisted of 16 battleships, seven destroyers, and four auxiliary ships. Here (from left), anchored off Coronado, are the warships *Kansas, New Jersey, Illinois,* and *Vermont.* (TI)

CALIFORNIA GOVERNOR James N. Gillett (hand on hat) came to San Diego to receive the fleet. In line behind Governor Gillett was the fleet's temporary commanding officer, Rear Adm. Charles M. Thomas, who filled in for the ailing Rear Adm. Robley D. "Fighting Bob" Evans. (TI)

AT NIGHTFALL, ships of the Great White Fleet, anchored off San Diego, were strung with electric lights. In an effort to match the dramatic display, San Diegans decorated their homes and business with lights, and built signal fires on the beaches. (TI)

[78]

MORE THAN sixteen thousand sailors hit San Diego, their pockets bulging with back pay. The city was decorated with flags and bunting, and the sailors were invited into homes for dinner. The Stingaree rolled out the red carpet and turned up the red lights. On April 15, 50,000 San Diegans and visitors crowded Broadway as 5,000 crewman marched to the accompaniment of military and local bands. Many crewmen and officers, so impressed by their first visit to San Diego, were to return later to make their homes in the city. It was a pattern that would be repeated with regularity over the next seven decades. (TI)

FRIDAY NIGHT FIGHTS in San Diego's first boxing arena, the Dreamland Boxing Club, 1907: Two of the sailors in the front row seem unimpressed by the match. They've found their own dreamland. (TI)

SAN DIEGOS FIRST PRIZE FIGHT ARENA - 1907
BILL D'COURSEY - REFEREE - IN THE CENTER

THE FIRST HOME of Scripps Institution of Oceanography, then called the Marine Biological Association of San Diego, was at Alligator Head, above the Cove Beach in La Jolla *(below)*. Dr. William E. Ritter *(left)*, head of the department of biology at the University of California, had surveyed the West Coast to locate the best spot for his biological work. He was persuaded by publisher E. W. Scripps and his sister, Ellen Browning Scripps, to locate at La Jolla. The big building is the La Jolla Bath House. The little, 24-foot by 60-foot shanty housed Ritter's laboratory and aquarium. (TI)

[79]

LA JOLLA'S GROWTH forced Ritter and his Marine Biological Association out of the Cove area in 1907, so Ellen Browning Scripps induced the city to sell the association a parcel of pueblo land at La Jolla Shores. The first building was erected in 1909, and Ritter, with his staff, moved in the next year. In 1912, the name was changed to Scripps Institution for Biological Research of the University of California, becoming a formal part of the university. In 1925, the name was changed a third time, to Scripps Institution of Oceanography. (TI)

[80]

THE NATURAL BEAUTY of San Diego brought unanimous praise from visitors. But few San Diegans believed the city's beauty could be translated into jobs, attracting the population needed to build a great city. Some, who had come to San Diego to retire peacefully, wanted San Diego to stand still, but they were a distinct minority. This was the essence of the "smokestacks versus geraniums" controversy. A few of the more farsighted among the city's leaders, like George Marston (left) and Ed Fletcher (center) believed San Diego could have both. It was Marston who persuaded John Nolen (right), a landscape architect from Massachusetts, to come to San Diego to design a unified plan for the city's development. (TI)

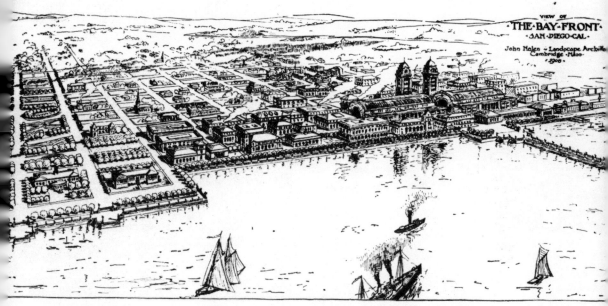

THE PLANNER NOLEN laid out a comprehensive design, putting all of San Diego's municipal buildings at the waterfront. He wrote at length about the fabulous natural assets of the community and how they should be incorporated into developing the great city that would surely rise around the waterfront. Nolen pointed out all of the missed opportunities of other cities that fronted on rivers or oceans, and begged San Diego not to forfeit its chance. He presented his plan to directors of the Chamber of Commerce in March 1908. The Chamber studied it a full ten months. When it finally released it to the public, in 1909, the public had lost interest, and it was buried under other city business. (TI)

[81]

FIRST IT HAD BEEN Alonzo Horton. Now, in the 1900s, San Diego was again becoming a one-man town. The man who replaced Horton was John Spreckels. By 1906, Spreckels, who had continued to reside in San Francisco, was seriously ill. Death, his family was warned, was imminent. After the San Francisco earthquake in April 1906, Spreckels and his family fled aboard his yacht to Coronado. His health returned, and Spreckels decided to construct a $100,000 home across the street from Hotel del Coronado. He would, he said, donate all his future energies to the development of San Diego and Coronado. (UT)

AFTER A RARE CLEANSING RAIN, the exploding metropolis of San Diego in 1912: San Diego continued to live in the shadow of Los Angeles, but there was promise. A railroad to the East, finally, seemed assured. Spreckels had bought out the San Diego & Eastern Railroad, established in 1902, and paid back everything subscribers had put up. He wanted no subsidies from any person or government, he said. He would do it all himself. But the railroad was still seven years away. It would be slowed by a world war, and cost far more than originally estimated. (TI)

SAN DIEGO WAS RIPE in the teen years of the twentieth century for all manner of entrepreneurs. One of the most infamous was C. H. Toliver, who arrived in 1911 with his wife, his dog Fritz, and his secretary, promising a new air machine that would replace railroads. He offered San Diegans a chance to get in on the ground floor, and the good citizens jumped. Toliver built his dirigible, a 250-foot-long and 40-foot-in-diameter white elephant with four gasoline engines and six propellers. He proposed to inflate it with hydrogen gas and take off with forty passengers on a flight that would astound the world. On November 11, 1911, it seemed all of San Diego had come to watch the air ship rise from its berth in a canyon at 31st and B streets. It never left the ground. The city, fearing the gas might explode, declared Toliver's dirigible a public nuisance. Later, Toliver's male secretary, Hubert Lewis, demanded the money Toliver had promised him for the scheme. When Toliver refused it, Lewis settled by shooting to death both Toliver and Toliver's wife. Lewis was acquitted of the murders when his attorney established, on shaky evidence, that Toliver had alienated the affections of Lewis' wife. (TI)

GROWING UP AND out, University Avenue in 1911 was extended east from the Georgia Street Bridge. (TI)

[83]

NEIGHBORING SAN DIEGO had a ringside seat for the revolution underway in Mexico in 1910. The Industrial Workers of the World (IWW), a radical labor organization founded in 1905 and dedicated to a socialist order, took up the cause of Francisco Madero, leader of the revolutionary forces in Mexico. The IWW sent money and arms across the border from San Diego to Madero, and Madero, relatively unconcerned with his revolutionaries at the border, dispatched the arms and money to eight men. The eight quickly captured the border town of Mexicali. It was enough of a victory to further impress the IWW, which began recruiting volunteers on the streets of San Diego to join the revolution. When revolutionary forces at Mexicali numbered 250, they marched on Tijuana. The defenders had few arms, and often just barricaded themselves inside buildings. (TI)

[84]

THE BATTLE RAGED for two days before the revolutionary forces, led by a Welsh soldier of fortune named Caryl Rhys Price, had won control of the border town and raised the red flag over the post office proclaiming "Land and Liberty." After an inspection tour, Price liberated all the money he could find and left for Los Angeles to "discuss strategy with supporters." From there he sent word to the revolutionaries that the cause was lost, and advised them to disband. Price went "Hollywood" a few years later, taking cowboy roles in wild-West films. (TI)

JACK MOSBY (center, standing), a deserter from the U.S. Marines, decided to take command of what remained of the revolutionary forces. He assembled 155 men and went out to meet a force of 560 Mexican Federal troops who were on the way up the coast from Ensenada. (TI)

GREATLY OUTNUMBERED, Mosby and his forces retreated across the border and surrendered to American officials. The men were temporarily incarcerated at Fort Rosecrans on Point Loma. Mosby, having been identified as a deserter from the Marines, was shot and killed during an escape attempt. (TI)

MOVING DAY, 1911: The Buckingham Hotel is dollied from Second and Broadway to its new home at First and A. (TI)

PIONEER AVIATOR Glenn H. Curtiss (center, kneeling), attracted by favorable year-round flying conditions, arrived in San Diego during the winter of 1910-1911. John Spreckels, a flying enthusiast, donated land to Curtiss on Coronado's North Island where Curtiss set up a flying school. Curtiss sent word to the Navy offering to train a few of its officers at no cost. At first, the offer was declined. But when Curtiss demonstrated that planes could be used successfully as scouting vehicles for ships at sea, the Navy accepted. The Navy not only sent officers for training, but also placed orders for Curtiss' planes. His school was not limited to military personnel, and many early aviators got their training here. (TI)

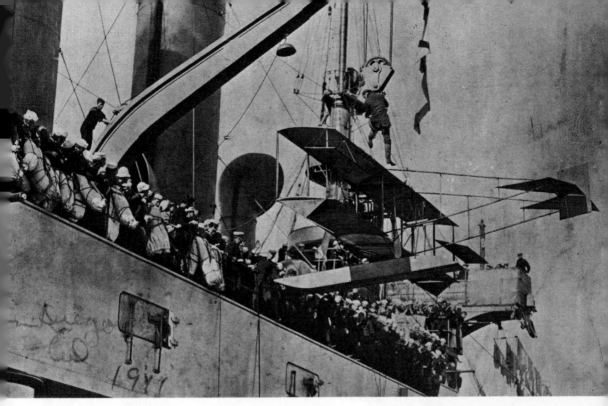

THE NAVY was impressed by Curtiss' demonstration that a plane could be launched from a ship, but wanted evidence that the plane, once launched, could be retrieved by a moving vessel. Curtiss designed a float that would sustain the airplane in water and, after a few practice runs, he took off from North Island and flew to the waiting U.S.S. *Pennsylvania.* He landed near the ship and was hoisted aboard by crane. The crane then lowered the plane to the water and Curtiss made the return flight to North Island. Satisfied with the demonstration, the Navy appropriated $25,000 for further development. (TI)

LIEUTENANT T. G. Ellyson was the first to be sent to North Island for training under Curtiss, and became the Navy's first aviator. (TI)

EUGENE ELY, a Curtiss employe, demonstrated the speed and maneuverability of the early biplanes to a crowd of 1,500 at Coronado's Polo Grounds in 1911. (TI)

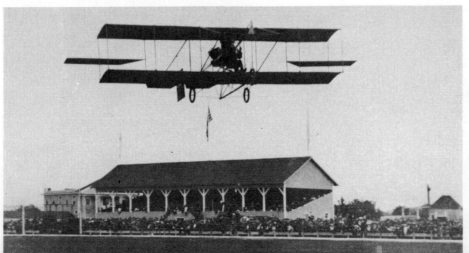

THE AERIAL CIRCUSES were part of Curtiss' efforts to awaken interest in flying. On January 28, 1911, in a race between Curtiss and Ely at the Polo Grounds, blinding speeds up to sixty miles per hour were reached. (TI)

AMONG THE NOTABLES of early aviation who came to San Diego to work with Curtiss was Dr. Albert F. Zahm, developer of the first wind tunnel. (TI)

HARRY HARKNESS, the New York millionaire flying enthusiast, arrived in San Diego in January 1911, to join in one of Curtiss' air shows, and took delivery of two of his crated Antoinette aeroplanes. During his stay, Harkness assisted the U.S. troops, stationed just above the Mexican border during the insurrection, by dropping messages from his plane. (TI)

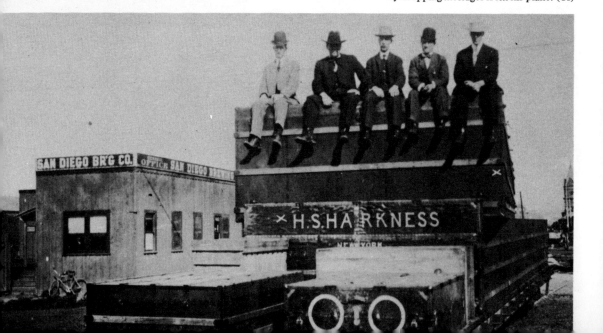

THE INDUSTRIAL WORKERS of the World, the socialist group attracted to San Diego during the Tijuana Insurrection, descended on the city in the hundreds in 1912 to protest an ordinance against street-corner speeches. The ordinance was passed specifically to discourage the Wobblies who were blocking entrances to businesses and sidewalks. With their reinforcements from Los Angeles, the Wobblies formed groups and made speeches in defiance of the ordinance. Twenty-four hours a day, somewhere in the city, they would step up on soap boxes and criticize the city and its policies. As one orator was arrested, another would take his place. Soon the jail was so crowded with IWW members, the prisoners had to be farmed out to Santa Ana, Riverside, and San Bernardino. The Wobblies outraged San Diegans, who converged on the jail, demanding they be run out of town. (TI)

FIREMEN WERE CALLED OUT, at one point, to disperse the Wobblies with fire hoses, and a battle raged for hours. The *Oakland World,* in an article sympathetic to the Wobblies and their free-speech movement, reported: "For a full hour hundreds packed themselves in a solid mass . . . bending themselves to the terrific torrent that poured upon them. They held their ground until swept from their feet by the irresistible flood. An old, gray-haired woman was knocked down by the direct force of the stream . . . a mother was deluged with a babe in her arms." Sympathetic news accounts further enraged San Diegans, some of whom formed vigilante groups to drive the Wobblies out. (TI)

EMMA GOLDMAN (with wide-brimmed hat), the woman anarchist who supported the IWW cause, arrived in San Diego when actions and reactions were at a fever pitch. The Wobblies claimed they had been taken in groups to Sorrento Valley where scores of men forced them to kiss the American flag or sing the National Anthem. Later, they said, they were taken to San Onofre, where they were made to run through double rows of men armed with clubs, whips, and guns, and were beaten repeatedly. Mrs. Goldman's arrival fanned the fires. After being driven by police escort to the U.S. Grant in the hotel's open-air bus, she was met by a group of men in her hotel room. They kidnapped her, she claimed, and took her out of town. Then, she said, she was subjected to the same tortures as the Wobblies. The Wobblies, who held the anarchists in contempt, would have no part of Mrs. Goldman. They accused her of running away from a crowd that was more interested in hissing her than harming her. With Mrs. Goldman's exit, though, the free-speech movement died out. (TI)

THE CATHOLIC SOCIETY of San Diego picnics at the ruins of the San Diego Mission in 1913. (TI)

POINT LOMA ROAD races were a wildly popular spectator sport in San Diego in the first two decades of the 1900s. W. H. Carlson won the "big car" event in the 200-mile race in March 1913. Driving a Benz, at speeds exceeding 100 miles per hour, he was in second place until the very end. The leader, an Italian driver named Tony Janette, blew his engine on the last leg. Janette later was quoted by *The San Diego Union:* "I never hada da luck." (TI)

THE WINNER of the "small-engine-displacement class' on March 1, 1913, at the Point Loma Race-track was "Spider" Campbell, who drove number 16, a Buick. Campbell was one of two drivers to finish the race. Third place went to the last car to break down. (UT)

THE COLDEST DAY on record in San Diego came on January 7, 1913, when the mercury dipped to 25 degrees, an Arctic temperature when compared to the usually-mild climate. Water in the Plaza fountain froze over, and youngsters tested it while the curious gathered to witness the freak of nature. (UT)

AN ATTENTION-GETTER was all San Diego needed to fulfill its destiny as a great city. With the completion of the Panama Canal in a few years, San Diegans told themselves, their city could become a principal port of call in a great new Atlantic-Pacific sea trade. An exposition would not only provide a major attraction for commerce, but would help develop the languishing City Park as well. Private subscriptions raised a million dollars and a bond issue was approved for an additional million dollars for park improvements. The City Park became Balboa Park in November 1910. The Panama-California Exposition Company selected a site in the southwest corner of the park, and ground breaking ceremonies were held on July 19, 1911. As the city's civic leaders stood by with pick and shovel, Pres. William Howard Taft pressed a button in the East Room of the White House which unfurled an American flag at the site of the ceremony. At center, two to the left of the man holding the pick, was banker G. Aubrey Davidson, who first conceived of a San Diego exposition.

DIRECTOR GENERAL D. C. Collier suggested an exposition in keeping with the culture of Southern California—a miniature city with buildings in the style of the missions, and gardens suggesting the atmosphere of Old Spain. The outbreak of World War I had a severe impact on building activity in San Diego, but the Expo went ahead on schedule. (UT)

BALBOA STADIUM was completed in 1914 as a major facility for special events of the 1915 Expo. The stadium cost $135,000 and seated 20,000. It was situated on the southeast corner of Balboa Park, and would be, for the next fifty-five years, the city's only public stadium. (TI)

THE PANAMA-CALIFORNIA Exposition's opening was set for midnight January 1, 1915, several weeks ahead of a planned World's Fair in San Francisco. The main approach was from the west over a newly constructed bridge spanning Cabrillo Canyon. It took time for word of the San Diego Expo to reach across the country, and early attendance figures were disappointing. Average daily attendance during January was 4,783. The next month it had dropped to 4,360. But later in the year, attendance shot upward, with thousands of visitors to San Francisco's fair coming south to San Diego. In October, a hundred prominent Los Angeles citizens, among them *Los Angeles Times* publisher Harrison Gray Otis, met with Expo officials and pledged $150,000 to keep the Panama-California Exposition going for another year. It was good business for Southern California. (TI)

AMONG THE FIRST dignitaries at San Diego's Expo were U.S. Vice Pres. Thomas Riley (center, left), and Asst. Sec. of the Navy Franklin Delano Roosevelt (center, right, with cane). Riley and Roosevelt flanked Expo Pres. G. Aubrey Davidson. Roosevelt used the occasion to announce that San Diego had been selected as the probable location for the Navy's West Coast dirigible base. (TI)

FORMER PRESIDENT Theodore Roosevelt visited the Expo in 1915 and toured the Indian Village. In an address that day, Roosevelt said, "It is so beautiful that I wish to make an earnest plea . . . I hope that not only will you keep these buildings of rare, phenomenal taste and beauty permanently . . . I hope that you of San Diego will recognize what so many other communities have failed to recognize: That beauty is not only well worthwhile for its own sake, but that it is valuable commercially." With attendance improving steadily during 1915, the decision was made to continue for a second year. By the end of the two-year run, total attendance topped three-and-a-half million. (TI)

THE STINGAREE, San Diego's grisly but highly popular collection of bars and whorehouses, was at its peak in 1912, a time when many San Diegans were concerned with presenting the best possible public image for the upcoming Expo. The Stingaree covered an area bounded by First, Sixth, Market, and the bay. Dozens of cribs lined the streets, particularly along Fourth. Saloons provided rooms upstairs, with entry through the rear door, marked with a red light. (TI)

KENO WILSON, San Diego's newly elected chief of police, posed in 1911 with Captain B. Moriarty and Chief Gonzalez, the 101-year-old first policeman of San Diego's New Town. Wilson, who opposed closing the Stingaree District, was under intense pressure. Wilson said he preferred having the red light district where police could keep an eye on things. Closing it, he said, would spread prostitution to the suburbs. (TI)

THE PRESSURE BECAME irresistible in the fall of 1912, and Chief Wilson yielded. In a mass arrest, on the evening of November 10, the chief and his men swept down on dozens of bawdy houses and cribs and rounded up 138 madams and prostitutes. After the bust, a half-dozen of San Diego's working girls posed in the city jail around a table laden with books, magazines, and the Holy Bible. The next morning, all 138 were lined up in front of Judge George Puterbaugh, one of those who had pressured for the raid, and were fined $100 each. Puterbaugh suspended the fine on the condition they leave the town "forthwith" and not return. (TI)

Facing page: THE STINGAREE RAID made page nine of *The San Diego Union,* with a story quoting Chief Wilson, who said, "The lid's on for good." The story notes that as many male customers as women were arrested, but that their arrests were "merely perfunctory," and they were released without booking. History does not record what became of the two prostitutes who agreed to reform, but many of the 136 who were trouped down to the Sante Fe Station to purchase tickets to Los Angeles, it was noted later, bought round-trip passage. Many slipped back into town quietly, turning up in large rented homes, in more respectable neighborhoods. The madams were now hostesses. (TI)

138 Women Are Arrested in Stingaree Raid

136 Promise To Leave City; Two Agree to Reform

Scenes Illustrating Stingaree Raid: Top, Leaving Home Under Guard; Next Below, Left, Unloading at Station; Right, Leading Wagon as Pretentious Resort. Next Below, Patrol Wagon Overflow Marching to Station. Bottom, Some Hid Their Face, From Camera Man.

We go to

San Francisco

every night

without change of cars
Santa Fe's new fast train
The Saint: From here 1:10 p. m. daily
offers you an evening of ease
and a night of rest—

The Angel: Brings you back.

Santa Fe

Hotels and Resorts

AMERICA'S LARGEST ALL YEAR RESORT

JOHN J. HERNAN, Manager.

AUTOMOBILISTS

The ideal auto trip of Southern California:—San Diego to Del Mar via La Jolla, and return via Miramar and Murphy Canyon. Fifty miles of excellent roads. Magnificent scenery the entire way

— Also —

THE STRATFORD INN
AT DEL MAR

WARNER HOT SPRINGS

The ancient Indian remedy for all diseases. "Marvelous cures."
F. S. SANDFORD, Mgr. Auto Service. Sunset 3484.

New Southern Hotel, Cor. 6th & B

U. S. Grant Hotel Bivouac Grill

Palomar Mt. Hotel

THE WILLOWS

AUTO STAGE

IMPERIAL

PRE-EMPT A FARM HOME

Paradise Valley Sanitarium

**RAPHAEL TUCK'S
PRIVATE XMAS CARDS—**

LORING'S BOOK STORE   761 FIFTH ST.

ONLY ONE COUPON REQUIRED

COUPON

Save it for a copy of

The American Government

By FREDERIC J. HASKIN

The Book That Shows Uncle Sam at Work

NOVEMBER 11

[97]

A MINOR RUBBISH fire turned into a blazing inferno on the night of October 5, 1913, when the Standard Oil Company's tanks were caught up in the flames. Fiery oil overflowed into the Whiting Mead lumber yard, destroying it. The flaming fuel found its way to San Diego Bay, where it burned on the water. Flames consumed all of Standard's storage tanks, with over a million gallons of various grades of oil. The loss was estimated at $400,000. The fire was battled for several days, at times endangering the entire city. (TI)

A NEW TRAIN DEPOT was built by the combined forces of the Santa Fe and the San Diego railways, and the old depot came down. The new depot was in keeping with the Spanish-style architecture of the Expo. (TI)

SAN DIEGO TRIED, in the early days of moving pictures, to match Hollywood's production for the fast-growing market, but never succeeded. Margarita Fisher, one of San Diego's early silent-screen personalities, filmed scenes for *The Little Girl Who Wouldn't Grow Up* on the beach in La Jolla. (TI)

SAN DIEGO FILMMAKERS on location at San Diego's Broadway Pier in 1919. (TI)

SPRECKELS THEATRE opened in August 1912, at a cost of more than a million dollars. It boasted a ten-ton, steel-and-asbestos fire curtain, and a six-story stage loft. A mountain was once constructed on stage for a production of *Old Arizona,* and mules were hoisted to the third floor so they could descend in pack trains. On another occasion, the theatre installed a treadmill for a live chariot race during a production of *Ben Hur.* (TI)

[100]

THE ARCHITECTURE and decorations of the Spreckels Theatre won wide acclaim. Among the notables who performed at the Spreckels were John Barrymore, Maude Adams, and Anna Held. (TI)

LA JOLLA, the jewel of the Pacific, in 1917, thirty years after the arrival of surveyor Frank T. Botsford, and twenty years after Anna Held began laying out her Green Dragon Colony. (TI)

THE STERN FACES of the San Diego
Rifle and Revolver Association atop the
roof garden of the U. S. Grant Hotel in
1915: That's Police Chief Keno Wilson,
standing, with the revolver pointed at
merchant Harry Hubbs. (TI)

A PLACE on the National Highway map was
essential to San Diego's dream of becoming a
great port city. San Diegans insisted the Yuma-
San Diego route was the most practical way
to reach the West coast from Phoenix. But
there were no through highways. A committee
headed by Ed Fletcher challenged Los Angeles
to a race, but before the race had been sanc-
tioned by the AAA, the *Los Angeles Exam-
iner* challenged the *Evening Tribune* to a
preliminary pathfinder race. San Diego's entry,
the "Tribune-Gazette," an air-cooled Franklin,
was driven by Fletcher through El Centro toward distant sand hills that had been studiously
avoided by others. But Fletcher had taken no
chances. Six horses had been stationed in the
hills along the way to free his auto when it
bogged down in the sand. He arrived in Phoenix 19½ hours after leaving San Diego. The Los
Angeles entry broke down in the desert near
Blythe and never reached Phoenix. (TI)

THE SANDHILLS that Fletcher labored so hard to cross, were the main barrier to traffic. They
could be avoided by a 46-mile detour, but that led traffic toward Los Angeles, and San Diego
was vying with Los Angeles to become the West Coast terminus of the Southern auto route. San
Diegans decided a plank road would prove that the shortest route west lay in the direction of
San Diego. The first spike was driven on Febraury 13, 1915, and in three weeks, a two-track
road had been laid across six miles of sand. It required steady hands to navigate the road, but
the plank road demonstrated that a modern highway could be successfully built across the
sands. (TI)

[102]

A PARCHED SAN DIEGO was ready to listen to anyone in 1915 who could promise the much-needed rain. The city's reservoir at Lake Morena was, by then, little more than a wading pool. On December 8, fearing a catastrophic drought, the City Council accepted almost certain public ridicule and contracted with a professed rainmaker by the name of Charles Hatfield (center). The rainmaker agreed to produce enough precipitation to fill the reservoir to the brim for $10,000. If he failed, he was to receive nothing. Left of Hatfield is his brother, Paul, and on his right is realtor Francis Binney. (TI)

HATFIELD SET UP shop at Morena Reservoir, erecting a tower topped by a twelve-foot plat-form. He began mixing his mysterious chemicals, which he claimed would coax the clouds to release the stored-up water. Meanwhile, a high pressure system was building over the Pacific Ocean and began moving south toward San Diego. Little thought was given to Hatfield and his chemistry until January 14, 1916, when a steady rain began to fall. By January 17, the San Diego River started overflowing its banks, flooding Mission Valley and bringing reports of washed-out bridges, drowning livestock, delayed or stranded trains, and downed wires. (TI)

A BREAK in the Sweetwater Dam sent millions of gallons of water rushing down the Sweetwater Valley, destroying bridges and railroad embankments. By January 29, the storm total had reached 35 inches at Morena. (TI)

[104]

RAINMAKER HATFIELD came out of the hills and into flood-wrecked San Diego on February 4, demanding payment. City officials refused, claiming the rains and floods had been an act of God. Later, Hatfield filed suit against the city, then offered to settle for $1,800. The city agreed to pay if Hatfield would assume responsibility for lawsuits against the city for flood damages totaling $3.5 million. Hatfield respectfully declined, but his original suit remained on file until 1938. San Diego heard no more from Hatfield after 1916. Years later, a play and movie, entitled *The Rainmaker*, were produced on his exploits. (TI)

MADAME SCHUMANN-HEINK, in one of her many concerts at Horton Plaza. Ernestine
Schumann-Heink, a former Metropolitan Opera Company star described by one critic as "the
greatest contralto of her day," and by another as "the ugliest woman who ever walked across
a stage," came to San Diego in 1912. William B. Gross, a former actor and land speculator who
had been trying to establish a colony of artists, induced her to stay by giving her property. At
the 1915 Expo, she drew a crowd of 28,000 to one performance. Born in 1861, Madame
Schumann-Heink continued performing until the age of seventy-one. She began an acting career
in the movies in 1936, but died before completion of her second film. (TI)

SAN DIEGO'S PLACE in military history was firmly rooted in World War I. When Congress
declared war on Germany in April 1917, San Diego was chosen as the site for the War Department's Army cantonment in the Southwest, where year-round outdoor training was practical.
Land was leased on Linda Vista Mesa. The Army's camp was to be Camp Kearny, honoring
Gen. Stephen Watts Kearny, who led American forces in California in the 1840s during the
war with Mexico. (TI)

IDEAL WEATHER attracted the military to San Diego during World War I. For years, the Army had tried to buy North Island, where the Signal Corps had established its flying school, but the Spreckels interests had refused to sell. A bill was introduced in Congress to take over the property and let the courts decide the worth, and San Diego's Congressman William Kettner helped carry it through the House. It was signed into law on July 30, 1917, and the Army base was named Rockwell Field, after Lt. Lewis C. Rockwell, a pioneer Army aviator who was killed in a test flight in 1912. Later in 1917, 524 acres of Rockwell Field were transferred to the Navy for use by the Naval Air Service. (UT)

[106]

THE FIRST ARMY PLANE from the new Rockwell Field landed at Camp Kearny in 1918. Construction costs at the camp totaled $3,500,000 and the facility trained men from California, Arizona, Nevada, New Mexico, and Utah, who comprised the 40th Division.(TI)

TANK SOLDIERS train at Camp Kearny in 1918. The camp covered 3,254 acres within the city limits and 9,466 adjoining acres in the county. (TI)

SAN DIEGO HIGH SCHOOL students called a strike on June 6, 1918, to protest the firing of their principal and several teachers. The teachers and principal had, the students said, been victims of political harassment by the Board of Education. The students, 1,800 strong, marched from the school to the Board of Education on Third Avenue. Finding no one there, the students marched to the City Stadium and resolved to stay away from classes until the board heard their grievances. (TI)

SIXTEEN DAYS AFTER the signing of the Armistice, on November 27, 1918, 212 planes from Rockwell and other nearby Southern California military aviation fields flew in massed formation over the city. The war had come to an end, but San Diego had just begun its life as a military city. With the close of World War I, Rockwell Field had 101 officers, 381 enlisted men, and 497 planes. The Navy had spent almost $2,000,000 on its Naval Air Station on North Island which had 40 officers, 110 student officers, and 800 enlisted men. (TI)

THE KNIGHTS of Columbus rolled out their "dreadnaught of the land" for the 5,000 sailors of the Pacific Fleet who returned to the Pacific Coast after the First World War. In addition to providing free lemonade and cigarets, the Knights staged two dances for the sailors, some of whom appeared so young it seemed they might have required parents' permission to attend. (TI)

WORLD WAR I flying ace Eddie Rickenbacker, before becoming a war hero, had established an international reputation in automobile racing. Following World War I, Rickenbacker returned to San Diego, where he took part in auto races on Point Loma, and went through the turns on Torrey Pines grade. (TI)

PLUGGING THE ILL-FATED League of Nations, Pres. Woodrow Wilson visited San Diego on September 19, 1919. He spoke in Balboa Stadium, which was filled to overflowing by a crowd of 50,000. Wilson waved aloft a copy of the League of Nations Covenant and said, "The heart of humanity beats in this document." It would be a "death warrant" to the children of the country should the U.S. reject participation in the league. (TI)

STALLED BY WAR, financial disasters, and floods, Spreckels needed twelve years to keep his word to the people of San Diego. A railroad to the East was, at last, a reality. On Admissions Day, 1907, Spreckels had driven a silver spike at the foot of Twenty-seventh Street to mark the beginning of the line. And on November 15, 1919, he drove the golden spike at Carrizo Gorge, marking completion of the San Diego, Arizona & Eastern Railroad. But there was more frustration ahead. Hard rains, just after completion, forced the closing of the line for eight months because of landslides. (TI)

EDWARD, PRINCE OF WALES and heir to the British Throne, arrived in San Diego during April 1920, on a goodwill tour aboard the British battleship *Renown*. He was greeted by San Diego's flamboyant Mayor Louis Wilde and his wife (left), and by California Gov. William D. Stephens. (TI)

AFTER A SALUTE by a crowd of 25,000 in the City Stadium, Prince Edward was entertained at a ball at Hotel del Coronado. Mayor Wilde, who considered his daughter's coming out at least as important as a visit by British royalty, held the ball in his daughter's honor. Sixteen years later, the prince was to abdicate the throne of the United Kingdom to marry Wallis Warfield, a divorcee who lived in Coronado at the time of his visit to San Diego. Both steadfastly denied rumors they had met in San Diego in 1920. (TI)

Coming of Age: 1920 to 1945

SAN DIEGO came out of World War I and into the Roaring Twenties an awkward adolescent, still searching for itself. And the search would take San Diego again through the familiar cycle of boom, bust and war.

The city's population had more than doubled during the decade from 1910 to 1920, giving it nearly 75,000 residents. And the ever-present real estate promoters would find willing investors during the next ten years, boosting the population to 174,000.

But San Diego continued to lose the race for population and commerce to Los Angeles, and San Diegans still looked to their natural harbor for the greatness they were sure must come.

Finally, it was clear that San Diego would never find its destiny as a commercial port. It would be the military that would provide the city with the bulk of its maritime commerce.

Despite land sale schemes, Chamber-of-Commerce advertising and a second international exposition, San Diego would not avoid the despair of a national Depression.

But the gradually building military and the peacetime pioneering of such aviators as Claude Ryan, B. F. Mahoney, Charles Lindbergh and Reuben H. Fleet, would keep San Diego from hitting bottom during the 1930s.

San Diego emerged from the great Depression ahead of much of the nation because it began tooling for war ahead of much of the nation.

And as the war in Europe and the Pacific began to rise, so did San Diego.

MISSION BEACH 1922
SAN DIEGO CALIFORNIA

JOHN D. SPRECKELS, whose Hotel del Coronado was San Diego's premier resort of the day, unveiled plans in 1922 for a $4,000,000 amusement center on the beach at Mission Beach. Spreckels backed his belief that San Diego's future lay in the tourist industry. (TI)

NATIVES AND TOURISTS flocked to Mission Beach and Spreckels' amusement center in June 1925. The center, bathhouse, and dancing casino were dedicated on the 75th anniversary of California's statehood. It was to be the beginning of a fabulous, Miami-like resort with hotel, water-sports stadium, and convention center. But these additions never materialized, and the amusement center was one of Spreckels' final developments. (TI)

AMONG THE SPECULATORS in San Diego land during the 1920s were the actress-sisters Constance, Norma, and Natalie Talmadge, who brought their Hollywood fortunes to San Diego and poured them into Talmadge Park, an East San Diego subdivision. The city's population had jumped from 74,000 in 1920 to more than 116,000 three years later. A housing shortage developed and land speculation was fast and furious. (TI)

[113]

SPRECKELS DIED on June 7, 1926, before completion of the fourteen-story John D. Spreckels Building at Sixth and Broadway, which was to have been his personal monument. In a characteristic display of corporate sentimentality, it was one of the first properties disposed of by the Spreckels interests following his death. (TI)

LA JOLLA WAS STILL a tiny, charming village in the early 1920s, but charm then, as now, had its price. Realtors were commanding up to $10,000 each for beach-front lots. (TI)

SAN DIEGO ZOO, one day to boast the world's largest wild animal collection, was begun on a small plot along Park Boulevard near Balboa Park. Animal cages lined the boulevard behind the Indian Village, a creation for the 1915-16 Panama-California Exposition. (TI)

[116]

BY THE EARLY 1920s, the San Diego Zoo had found a permanent home inside Balboa Park. Ellen Browning Scripps, sister of publisher E. W. Scripps, and a philanthropist with no lack of business acumen, helped provide fences, and the zoo began charging visitors. (TI)

THE ZOO EXPANDED during the 1920s with donations from around the world. The little zoo, founded by Dr. Harry Wegeforth in 1916, was about to roar. (TI)

THE DEBATE over smokestacks or geraniums was moot in the early 1920s. Though San Diegans seemed oblivious, the Army and Navy were plotting the city's future. Naval Hospital, shown here, was dedicated in 1922, on the southeast border of Balboa Park. (TI)

THOUGH SHIPPING had been on the decline, work was begun on a second San Diego pier in 1922. But by completion of the pier, tonnage had increased enough to support it, and San Diego was becoming an important port city at last. (UT)

THE LUXURIOUS WHITE sister ships *Yale* and *Harvard* called regularly at the port of San Diego in the 1920s. Both passenger and freight service grew rapidly, with the value of shipping jumping from $19,000,000 in 1920 to more than $35,000,000 in 1925. (TI)

PROHIBITION in the United States transformed the dusty Mexican border town of Tijuana into a tourist mecca, with more than seventy-five bars and bistros operating at once, and such blantant lures as "the longest bar in the world." (TI)

AGUA CALIENTE RESORT, built in 1928 at a cost of $10,000,000, catered to the film colony and other free-spenders of the era. In its day, the high-life of Southern California swirled as much around Agua Caliente as it does today around Las Vegas. (TI)

UNTIL MEXICO'S ban on gambling in 1935, Hollywood stars and underworld figures gambled with abandon in the famed Gold Room casino. (TI)

THIRSTY CROWDS traveled railways and highways to pay tribute to the new Tijuana. Excited with booze and frenzied with the carnival tempo, they descended on Tijuana's racetrack. On re-opening day in January 1920, heavyweight champion Jack Dempsey served as honorary race starter. Sharing the carnival scene were movie stars of the day Charlie Chaplin, Tom Mix, Fatty Arbuckle, and Buster Keaton. (TI)

AN INTERNATIONAL INCIDENT was touched off in 1926 when Mr. and Mrs. Thomas Peteet and their two daughters were found dead in their San Diego home. The family, it was learned later, had been in Tijuana the night before where the girls were kidnapped, drugged, and molested. Returning home, the family turned on the gas, lay down, and waited to die, choosing suicide over disgrace. The U.S. Government ordered the border closed each night, and Baja California Governor Abelardo Rodriguez shut down fifty-two of the city's saloons. The chief of police and seven others were indicted in the Peteet case, but were never convicted. The border re-opened, as did most of the saloons. (TI)

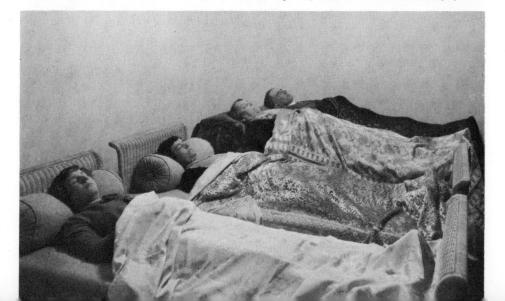

AVIATION was booming along with the twenties. Army and Navy pilots were charting the future of flight at Coronado's North Island. In 1922, a sustained-flight record was set by Army lieutenants Oakley Kelley and John Macready: 35 hours, 18 minutes. The next year, the first successful refueling in flight took place over San Diego when lieutenants Virgil Hine and Frank Seifert dropped a fuel line to John Richter's plane. (TI)

STUNT FLIERS made their fortunes and suffered their fractures in and around San Diego. On the beach in front of Coronado's Tent City, Clyde Pangborn attempted to board a plane by ladder from the back of a moving car. . .

. . . and failed. (TI)

THE FIRST lighter-than-air transcontinental flight ended in San Diego in 1924, when the Navy brought the dirigible *Shenandoah* to North Island. (TI)

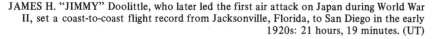

JAMES H. "JIMMY" Doolittle, who later led the first air attack on Japan during World War II, set a coast-to-coast flight record from Jacksonville, Florida, to San Diego in the early 1920s: 21 hours, 19 minutes. (UT)

T. CLAUDE RYAN, a young army pilot intent on a career in commercial aviation, came to Rockwell Field in 1922. As a reservist, Ryan could put in flying time and plot his commercial enterprise. By the end of the year, this was it. It consisted of one war-surplus "Jenny," an office in a piano box he picked up for a few dollars, and a runway at the foot of Broadway. (TR)

[123]

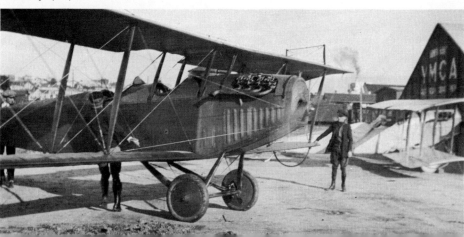

HIS FIRST EFFORT a spectacular failure, Ryan gave up the Broadway operation and took a job with a barnstorming expedition in Mexico. But with the money he earned, he bought some ancient government biplanes and reopened commercial operations on Dutch Flats, opposite the Marine Corps base. (TR)

RYAN CONVERTED his government biplanes into cabin transports, picked up a partner, B. Franklin Mahoney, and organized Ryan Airlines. On March 1, 1925, they began regular daily passenger service on the "Los Angeles-San Diego Airline." (TR)

EARLY THE FOLLOWING YEAR, Ryan's San Diego-to-Los Angeles airline boasted fifteen planes. But Ryan was dissatisfied with the planes available, and set about designing a new high-wing monoplane. The first, the M-1, was produced in ninety days and tested in February 1926. A few months later came Ryan's modified Brougham, shown here. By the end of the year, Ryan had sold his interest to his partner, Mahoney, but stayed on as general manager. (TI)

RYAN M-1 MONOPLANE

With 150 Hisso motor, $3750; with 180 Hisso motor, $4000;
with Wright Whirlwind motor, $8100.

RYAN BROUGHAM *(Five Place)*

With 180 Hisso motor, $5100; with Wright Whirlwind motor, $9700.

All prices at San Diego — Wire or write for convincing performance details.

RYAN AIRLINES, Inc., - SAN DIEGO, CALIFORNIA

ADVERTISEMENTS for Ryan's M-1 and Brougham reached St. Louis and twenty-five-year-old
mail pilot Charles Lindbergh in 1927. Lindbergh already had dreams of making the first non-stop
transatlantic flight and picking up $25,000 in prize money. He had obtained the needed financial
backing, but had been unable to find a suitable plane. Lindbergh visited Ryan's San Diego plant, and
inspected the first Brougham, *The Gold Bug,* then under construction. On February 27, he contracted
with Ryan Airlines to build him a modified version for the flight. Lindbergh took a room in San Diego
and watched over construction of the $10,000 aircraft. (TI)

[125]

FULLY ASSEMBLED, the *Spirit of St. Louis* was taken on its first test flight, with Lindbergh at the controls. The plane with a 46-foot wing span had been constructed in exactly two months, and workers had to labor around the clock for seven days a week in order to meet the deadline. (TI)

[126]

LINDBERGH FLEW the *Spirit of St. Louis* out of San Diego at 3:55 p.m. on May 10. He landed in St. Louis at 8:20 the next morning, and left for New York a day later. On the morning of May 20, he took off for Paris. His landing, 39½ hours later at Le Bourget Field, is history. (TI)

AFTER COMPLETING maneuvers off the California coast in March 1925, 120 battleships, scout cruisers, submarines, and destroyers descended on San Diego Harbor. San Diego was fast becoming a Navy city. (TI)

MISS SAN DIEGO hopefuls pose on the sand at Mission Beach in 1926. The roller skates were less a novelty than the bathing suits, which were particularly daring for the day. (UT)

COLONEL IRA C. COPLEY of Aurora, Illinois (left), a frequent visitor to San Diego, purchased *The San Diego Union* and *Tribune* from the Spreckels interests in 1928. He also bought the Spreckels home on Coronado, where he entertained such guests as Secretary of Commerce and future-president Herbert Hoover (second from right). (UT)

[128]

MORE THAN SIX INCHES of rain fell on San Diego in three days during February 1927, flooding the San Diego River and washing out highways, bridges, and railroad tracks. Train service to the city was suspended for six days, and Navy boats carried mail to and from Los Angeles. (TI)

THE ARCHED ROOF of the San Diego Trust and Savings Bank makes a fitting frame for a view of Broadway looking east from Sixth Avenue, taken in 1928, just before the Great Depression. (TI)

[129]

A GREAT TRANSPORTATION center requires a municipal airport, so San Diegans passed a $650,000 bond issue in 1927 to deepen the bay and use the fill to reclaim tidelands near Dutch Flats. An airport on the tidelands, within minutes of the downtown business district, was one of the suggestions of planner John Nolen, whom the citizens of San Diego had called on for a second time in 1925 to develop a design for the city's orderly growth. (TI)

[130]

MAJOR COMMERCIAL AIRLINES would continue to use Ryan Field on Dutch Flats for two years, though Lindbergh Field was officially dedicated on August 16, 1928, with Lt. Gov. Buron Fitts (far right) presiding. UT)

SING FIRST FLAG
ATE COLLEGE SITE,
SAN DIEGO·CAL. OCT. 7·1929.

INTEREST IN the Nolen Plan, met with little enthusiasm twenty years earlier, was revived in the 1920s through the efforts of businessman George Marston. The new plan drawn up by Nolen with funds from the City Council, grouped all public buildings on the waterfront along Harbor Drive. Balboa Park would be developed further, strictly for recreational use. One of the first tests of Nolen's second plan came immediately, when a new site was sought for San Diego Teachers' College (formerly San Diego Normal School). A proposal to build the new college in Balboa Park, on all remaining undeveloped acreage, was defeated by a 2-1 vote in a city election. It was a major victory for the Nolen Plan, one of few. Subsequently, a site was chosen in an area near Talmadge Park, overlooking Mission Valley and the San Diego Mission. (TI)

A THREE-DAY CEREMONY marked dedication of the first buildings at San Diego State University in May 1931. A Spanish official, a guest at the dedication, called the new college the finest example of Spanish architecture outside of Spain. (TI)

THE ORPHEUM, begun as the Pantages in 1924, and later taken over by RKO Pictures, featured silent films, talkies, and vaudeville, starring such greats as Ted Lewis, Jimmy Durante, Olson and Johnson, and Sophie Tucker. The Orpheum played live shows as late as 1951, when Lou Holtz brought in a musical revue. It was later razed to make room for a bank building. (UT)

THE STYLE SETTERS–girls of Gamma Delta Sigma sorority in 1929. (TI)

AS SAN DIEGO GREW out, it was also growing up. This photograph, taken in 1929 from North Island, shows the city's skyline as it would appear, virtually unchanged, for the next twenty-five years. (TI)

[133]

SAN DIEGO — CORONADO BRIDGE

A BRIDGE TO Coronado, envisioned by John D. Spreckels, was approved by the County Board of Supervisors in 1926. It was to cost $2,400,000 and the Spreckels Securities Company was to consult the Army Corps of Engineers. But with Spreckels' death, the bridge never materialized, and it would be more than forty years before San Diego and Coronado were linked by a bridge across the bay. (TI)

SCREEN COMEDIENNE Mildred Vincent, at the beck of the San Diego Chamber of Commerce, posed for promotional advertising advocating San Diego-grown grapefruit. (TI)

A PLETHORA of yellowfin and albacore tuna was to be found in the waters off San Diego and down the coast of Baja California. The catches of the fishing colony, dominated by Portuguese, were a major factor in the local canning industry which, in 1920, packed more than 250,000 cases of tuna. In 1925, more than 22 million pounds of albacore were landed. But the next year, for reasons unexplainable, the highly valued, white-meat albacore began disappearing from the California coast. While the fishermen searched fruitlessly for albacore in the warmer waters off Mexico, they began discovering vast resources of yellowfin and skipjack, the light-meat tuna which grew in economic importance. The year the albacore disappeared, tuna fishermen caught more than 45,000,000 pounds of other varieties of tuna in the waters off California and Baja California. The huge yellowfin often required three or four poles to land. (TI)

[135]

THE STATELY SPANISH buildings in Balboa Park were in a state of decay by the mid-twenties. There was talk of restoration, but nothing had been done to preserve the temporary facilities erected for the 1915-16 Exposition. A few hours before a scheduled firemen's ball on November 25, 1925, the original Southern California Counties Building (the converted civic auditorium) where the ball was to be held, caught fire. By the time firemen arrived, the building was destroyed. (UT)

MAKESHIFT TOUR BUSES ferried visitors to Balboa Park's Society of Natural History, the oldest scientific organization in Southern California. (UT)

HIGH FASHION and the local Tedlick Company's new fall line of ready-to-wear in 1927. (TI)

EL CORTEZ HOTEL was a new height of elegance for San Diego in 1927. Built by Dick Robinson and Associates at a cost exceeding $2,000,000, it replaced the home of U. S. Grant, Jr., at Seventh and Ash. (TI)

SAN DIEGANS celebrated the founding of the first Franciscan Mission on Presidio Hill with the dedication of Presidio Park and Museum on July 16, 1929. The park and museum were among George W. Marston's many gifts to the people of San Diego. Architect William Templeton Johnson designed the museum. (TI)

ELLEN BROWNING SCRIPPS built her elaborate home and gardens (foreground) on La Jolla's Prospect Street at the turn of the century. Her charities were legion. Among them were the Scripps Institute of Oceanography, the La Jolla's Women's Club (across Prospect from her estate), the Children's Playground and Community Center, a sanitarium which became Scripps Memorial Hospital, Scripps Clinic and Research Foundation, Hospitality House at Camp Kearny, a huge section of Torrey Pines Park, the tower and chimes for Saint James Episcopal Church, the San Diego Zoo, and the Bishop's School. (UT)

BENEFACTRESS Ellen Browning Scripps on her 94th birthday in 1930.

A VICTORIOUS CHARLES Lindbergh, who had successfully completed the non-stop transatlantic flight in a Ryan monoplane, returned to San Diego on September 2, 1927, to a hero's welcome. Lindbergh rode in a motorcade through city streets, with huge throngs jamming the entire parade route. In the City Stadium *(above)* a record crowd of sixty thousand turned out to pay tribute to Lucky Lindy. (TI)

[139]

THERE WERE HINTS of the Depression around the corner in 1928. Building permits had dropped dramatically, and arrivals of new residents, which had averaged 10,000 a year for the past six years, slipped to 2,000. But San Diegans were still pushing real estate. On Point Loma, the John P. Mills Company was subdividing and offering Mediterranean-style homes that ranged from $5,000 to $25,000. Developers of La Jolla Hermosa (shown here) advertised quick cash profits to investors. (UT)

THE STOCK MARKET CRASH of 1929 had little immediate effect on San Diego, but by 1930, building permits were cut by half again, and the newspaper's published list of tax delinquencies covered 64 pages. By 1931, San Diego was deep in the Depression. Food lines and a few public works projects helped lessen the ills of unemployment, but by 1932, 16,000 San Diegans were out of work. The city's total population was 223,000. Bank closings and bankruptcies were commonplace that year, and unemployment had jumped to 23,000 by 1933. (TI)

SOLAR AIRCRAFT COMPANY, with Edmund T. Price as president produced a new line of all-metal planes in 1931. But the aviation industry had been hit hard by the Depression, and despite lavish promotional attempts, Price could find no buyers. Solar, for a time, was forced to turn to production of kitchen utensils for the Navy. (UT)

U.S. NATIONAL BANK was one of the local banking institutions to survive the early Depression. Following President Roosevelt's national bank holiday in March 1933, U.S. National reopened. It had been taken over by a group headed by C. Arnholt Smith. Smith *(right)*, who had been a messenger during the 1920s, became an officer with Bank of America before taking control of U.S. National. The bank would remain in Smith's hands until 1973 when it would be declared insolvent in one of the nation's largest bank failures. (TI)

HARLEM AFTER DARK, featuring Dorothy Yoes and the Creole Cuties, at San Diego's Creole Palace, entertained a depressed San Diego in the 1930s. (TI)

RUTH ALEXANDER, a young aviatrix who had been flying less than a year, attempted a cross-country flight from San Diego to New Jersey in 1930. She held the women's altitude record that year, but when she took off from Lindbergh Field, she failed to clear Point Loma, and was killed in the crash. (TI)

THE U.S.S. *Langley,* the Navy's first aircraft carrier, called at San Diego's North Island in the late twenties and early thirties. (TI)

DOWNTOWN SAN DIEGO in 1933: Pre-traffic signals, post-traffic jams. (TI)

THE CITY, Coronado, and Point Loma, from the tower of the newly completed El Cortez Hotel in 1928. (TI)

INFORMATION ANDERSON was a fixture at Horton Plaza for thirty-three years. Adolph H. Anderson was hired by the San Diego Electric Railway Company in 1915 as a public relations gesture. He would answer, or find the answer, to any question posed. When he retired in 1948, a company spokesman figured Anderson had answered some 22,000,000 questions, 75 percent for the benefit of the community in general, and 25 percent for the railway company. (UT)

DEPRESSION AT HOME and a rising war in Europe sparked a Communist demonstration in San Diego in 1933. The Communists applied for a parade permit, but the city denied it. On May 30, they gathered at New Town Park and denounced San Diego's role in the military, the free-enterprise system and the ruling class. (TI)

THE 300 DEMONSTRATORS, all representatives of the Young Communist League of Angeles, attempted to parade without a permit and were met by police. A riot ensued and thirty demonstrators were injured. Two of suffered broken bones, eight of the Communists were jailed, and the others took their wounded and left town. (TI)

SAN DIEGO BAY, which had been dredged to provide tidelands fill for Lindbergh Field, was opened in the early 1930s to the biggest ships of the U.S. Navy. The aircraft carrier *Saratoga* steamed into San Diego Harbor on November 7, 1931, firing a 13-gun salute for Rear Adm. Thomas Senn, commandant of the 11th Naval District. The *Saratoga* was 888 feet long and carried a crew of 2,000. (UT)

THE SAN DIEGO MISSION, in tragic disrepair, underwent a partial facelifting in 1931. (UT)

HARD TIMES were well illustrated in 1934 by the San Diego Club's Billion Dollar Gold Room, a private dining room redecorated with worthless stock certificates. The club, organized in 1928 by Ed Fletcher as the San Diego Athletic Club, occupied a 14-story building on Sixth Avenue. (TI)

[146] DEEP IN THE DEPRESSION, and desperately seeking a way out, San Diego planned a second exposition in the mid-1930s. Restoration of the decaying 1915-16 Panama-California Exposition buildings had been undertaken in early 1933, and was nearly complete by the middle of 1934. Those buildings, it was decided, could be used to house many of the exhibits for the new Expo. With pledges of support from the federal government, and $700,000 in local subscriptions, the California Pacific International Exposition was launched. (TI)

NEW STRUCTURES were designed to blend with buildings of the first Expo, with architectural style progressing from native American Southwest and Mexican Aztec to modern. Industry, at first, was slow in committing itself to the exposition. Then, just four months before the scheduled opening, the Ford Motor Company agreed to participate, and other industries hurriedly followed suit. (TI)

ON OPENING DAY, May 29, 1935, sixty thousand persons attended the Expo, but the crowd was far below expectations. The average daily attendance during the first week was less than forty-five thousand. When an advertising campaign was launched, concentrating on California, and Los Angeles in particular, attendance began to swell. A huge midway featured an exhibit glamorizing the gangsters of the era—though it advertised: *Crime Never Pays*—with a display of John Dillinger's bullet-proof limousine. (TI)

GOLD GULCH, a simulated Western mining town in one of the park's many canyons, was a popular feature with fairgoers. It was also popular with police, who patrolled it regularly to control illegal gambling activities. In addition to the simulated mining town of Gold Gulch, the Expo featured a simulated nudist colony, which proved equally popular. (TI)

TOWARD THE END of the Expo's first year, Pres. and Mrs. Franklin Roosevelt visited San Diego. At a rally in the City Stadium on October 2, Roosevelt pointed to the exposition as evidence of an economic turnabout. In November it was decided to continue the Expo for a second year. But if economic recovery was just around the corner in 1935, the 1936 run of the exposition would offer little proof. Many exhibitors either downgraded or cancelled their displays, and attendance never matched first-year levels. The Expo closed on September 9, 1937, with a two-year attendance of 7,220,000. (UT)

THE VOLLEYBALL TEAM of the San Diego Club was on its way to another national championship match in 1937. Playing under official A.A.U. sanction, it had won the U.S. national amateur championship in a tournament staged in San Diego in 1935 during the Exposition. (TI)

LANE FIELD, the first home of Pacific-Coast-League team, the San Diego Padres, was built by the Harbor Commission and Works Progress Administration at the foot of Broadway in 1936. Ted Williams, one of baseball's greatest hitters, broke into organized baseball with the Padres that year, batting .271. The field was converted to harbor warehouse facilities in 1957. (UT)

FOUR TIMES San Diegans had rejected bond issues to provide a new civic center, but finally, in 1935, federal money assured its construction. The center was to be built on the waterfront site suggested a decade earlier by John Nolen. A group headed by George Marston, G. Aubrey Davidson, and Julius Wagenheim got assurances of $300,000 in WPA funds and a promise of more. The artist's conception of the center looks very much like the finished complex. which was dedicated in 1938 by President Roosevelt. (TI)

MAJOR AND MRS. Reuben H. Fleet. (UT)

AFTER SURVEYING each city in the country with a population greater than 100,000, Reuben H. Fleet, president of Consolidated Aircraft Corporation of Buffalo, New York, decided to relocate his operations in Southern California. In the end it was weather, once again, that worked in San Diego's favor. Consolidated's chief product was a Navy seaplane, and Lindbergh Field, with its proximity to the harbor, clinched the choice. Consolidated arrived in San Diego with $9,000,000 in back orders in 1934, and the work force doubled in the first year. The first planes were delivered by the end of 1935. Consolidated's original San Diego plant, on Pacific Highway just north of Lindbergh Field, was 900 feet long and 300 feet wide. (TI)

THE DEL MAR RACETRACK was born at the height of the Depression in 1937, when the WPA advanced $500,000 to the 22nd Agricultural District to build a county fairgrounds, grandstand, and track. A franchise for racing had been granted to crooner Bing Crosby in 1936 and a board of directors, including Crosby, actor Pat O'Brien, and Oliver Hardy was elected at Warner Brothers Studios on May 6, 1936. (TI)

ON OPENING DAY, July 3, 1937, thirty-three-year-old Crosby took to the turnstile, accepting tickets for the racetrack's premiere season. (DM)

COMEDIAN W. C. FIELDS entertained the jockeys "Where the Surf Meets the Turf." (DM)

[152]

ACTOR ANDY DEVINE and La Jollan Norris Goff posed with their catch after a San Diego fishing trip in 1939. Devine and Goff starred with Chester Lauck in the CBS Radio series "Lum & Abner." (TI)

HAVING LONG SINCE established the value of its year-round temperate climate for training, San Diego was bristling with military enclaves in 1941. Camp Callan received its first draftees for anti-aircraft training that year. Closed soon after the war, Callan's site now encompasses the University of California at San Diego, the Salk Institute, and Torrey Pines Golf Course. The main Pacific Highway between San Diego and Los Angeles passed hard by Camp Callan. (TI)

WITH THE UNITED STATES' entry into World War II inevitable, an anti-aircraft unit of the 216th Coast Artillery was assigned to guard one of the buildings of the Consolidated Aircraft Corporation in 1941. It was a practice maneuver, Army officers said, and would last an indefinite period. But similar units were placed on the roofs of other buildings at the plant. Six months later, with the bombing of Pearl Harbor by the Japanese, the U.S. was at war. And San Diego's vast military establishment made it seem a prime target. (UT)

WORKERS AT Consolidated Aircraft are urged on to greater productivity for the war effort in 1942. (TI)

AS THE TEMPO of the war quickened in the Pacific, the Navy established Camp Elliot on Kearny Mesa as a training center for the Marines of the Pacific Fleet. The first recruits arrived in June 1941. At the peak of the war, Camp Elliott was training 16,000 men a month for island fronts. (TI)

THE PBY CATALINA flying boat, which was first produced in 1932, carried a major share of Navy combat action in the early months of the Pacific war. Produced by Consolidated, the Catalina was the basic patrol plane of the Navy. An amphinian version of the Catalina, the PBY 5-A shown here, was known as the work horse of the Navy. (UT)

MORE THAN 200 PB2Y Coronado patrol bombers *(below),* the larger and more sophisticated outgrowths of the Catalina, were produced by Consolidated in San Diego for use during World War II. The model shown taxiing on San Diego Bay was a PB2Y-3R, a transport version of the Coronado. (UT)

[155]

CITY LIGHTS: Post World War II San Diego, and a skyline barely changed in 25 years. (TI)

POSTWAR San Diego, August 14, 1945, after the announcement of the surrender of Japan. The city that had so yearned for recognition had become a crowded staging area for World War II. The population in 1945 passed 300,000, and San Diego, as a military bastion, had stepped out of the shadow of Los Angeles. (UT)

THE END OF THE WAR left behind thousands of veterans who had discovered San Diego and decided to make it their home. But jobs were scarce and the city would have to find new ways of employing its people. (TI)

HONORING THE WAR DEAD at Fort Rosecrans National Cemetery on Point Loma. (UT)

Bibliography

Booth, Larry, Roger Olmstead and Richard F. Pourade, *Portrait of a Boom Town—San Diego in the 1880s.* San Diego: from the California Historical Society with the assistance of James S. Copley and Copley Books, 1971.

Riggins, Shelley J., and Richard Mansfield, *This Fantastic City—San Diego.* City of San Diego, 1956.

Hopkins, H. C., *History of San Diego: Its Pueblo Lands & Water.* San Diego: City Printing Company, 1929.

Lockwood, Herbert, *Skeleton's Closet.* Bailey and Associates, 1973.

McPhail, Elizabeth C., *The Story of New San Diego and of Its Founder, Alonzo E. Horton.* San Diego: Elizabeth C. McPhail, 1969.

Pourade, Richard F., *The Explorers.* San Diego: The Union-Tribune Publishing Company, 1960.

Pourade, Richard F., *Time of the Bells.* San Diego: The Union-Tribune Publishing Company, 1961.

Pourade, Richard F., *The Silver Dons.* San Diego: The Union-Tribune Publishing Company, 1963.

Pourade, Richard F., *The Glory Years.* San Diego: The Union-Tribune Publishing Company, 1964.

Pourade, Richard F., *Gold in the Sun.* San Diego: The Union-Tribune Publishing Company, 1965

Pourade, Richard F., *The Rising Tide.* San Diego: The Union-Tribune Publishing Company, 1967

Randolph, Howard S. F., *La Jolla Year by Year.* La Jolla: The Library Association of La Jolla, 1955.

Smythe, William E., *History of San Diego.* San Diego: William E. Smythe, 1908.

Wagner, William, and Lee Dye, *Ryan, the Aviator.* New York: McGraw-Hill, 1971.

Index of Names

by E. S. Glover and Published by Schneider & Kueppers, San Diego.

Entered according to Act of Congress, in the year

Showing the central portion of the city, with the *actual* improvements; San Diego Bay and Peninsula, the Entrance
to the Harbor, Point Loma, and the Los Coronados Islands, twenty miles distant
in the Pacific Ocean.

1. Presbyterian Church.	5. Catholic Church.	9. Bank of San Diego.
2. Baptist Church.	6. Public Schools.	10. Commercial Bank.
3. Methodist Church.	7. Point Loma Seminary.	11. City Hall.

BIRD
SAN DIEG